PRAISE FOR *THE LAST LA...*
"Poignant and powerful. One family's history comes ...
sharp focus against the tragic events of the present."
OLGA WOJTAS

PRAISE FOR *A PROPER PERSON TO BE DETAINED*
"Turns difficult family subject matter into a fascinating
book, full of resonance." IRISH TIMES

"An emotional journey into a family's past ... written with
empathy, insight and warmth." FAMILY TREE MAGAZINE

"A champion of the under-represented, overlooked, and
persecuted, Czerkawska is rightly known as one of the
most interesting and individual historical novelists we
have, able to find a relatable way to tell a story that may
have been overlooked otherwise." SCOTS WHAY HAE

PRAISE FOR HISTORICAL NOVELS
"Finally gives voice to Jeany Armour ... who was muse,
mother, wife and lover to Scotland's national poet. This is
her song." SUNDAY MAIL

"The characters are finely drawn and believable... I was
entranced." HISTORICAL NOVELS REVIEW

"Czerkawska tells her tale in a restrained, elegant prose."
SUNDAY TIMES HISTORICAL NOVELS OF THE MONTH

Published by Saraband
3 Clairmont Gardens,
Glasgow, G3 7LW, UK

ISBN: 9781913393670

Printed and bound in Great Britain by Clays Ltd, Elcograf S.p.A.

1 2 3 4 5 6 7 8 9 10

Page ii: The Czerkawski Family at Dziedziłow, 1929.
Opposite: Władysław Czerkawski.

The Last Lancer

A Story of
Loss and Survival
in Poland and Ukraine

Catherine Czerkawska

Saraband

For my grandfather,
Lancer Władysław Czerkawski
14th January 1904 – 30th July 1942
From Kasia with love.

Above: Anna Brudzewska von Brause and Łucja Czerkawska.

Below: Julian in childhood, before everything changed.

Into my heart an air that kills
From yon far country blows:
What are those blue remembered hills,
What spires, what farms are those?

That is the land of lost content,
I see it shining plain,
The happy highways where I went
And cannot come again.

A E HOUSMAN

'So let us tell you this – you will never understand us, and how the experiences of multiple occupations shaped our societies, and how that historical experience is present in our everyday conversations and in our system of values. In our part of Europe, everyone has had beef with each other, and we are raised with that knowledge about each other. There are CENTURIES of beef between Poland and Ukraine, centuries of bloody and painful history. We put it all aside on day ONE of the Russian invasion.'

POLISH LEFTISTS ON FACEBOOK

EASTERN EUROPE IN 1918 AND TODAY

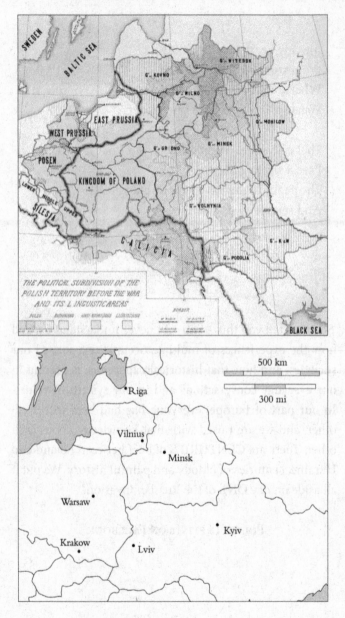

Contents

Family Tree: One

Paweł Czerkawski of Meryszczów in Galicia m Eufrozyna Podlesiecka
172?

Antoni Czerkawski m Marianna Kulpińska
b 1739 b 176?

Benedict Czerkawski m Maria Ścisłowska
b 1763 d 1833
d 1852

Andrzej — Michał — Katarzyna — Ignacy Michał — Jan — Józef — Maria — Anna — Aleksander
b 1789   b 1792   b 1795   b 1797   b 1799   b 1802   b 1807   b 1808   b 1810
                                          (died in   d 1882
                                          infancy)

m Antonina
Dobrowolska

m
Aniela
Żukowska 1827

Julia   Emilia

Julian Czerkawski
b 1831
d 1911
at Dziedziłów

Władysław Jan Paweł — Stanisław m Helena Leopoldyna Wanda
b 1829?   b 1831   Dobrowolska
                               185?

m. Maria Walitschek   Helena Czerkawska
1855   b 185?

Władysław Norbert Włodzimierz Czerkawski m Fryderyka Rosa Mick 187?
b at Meryszczów in 1856
d 1910?

Julian Władysław Benedykt
b 187?

Family Tree: Two

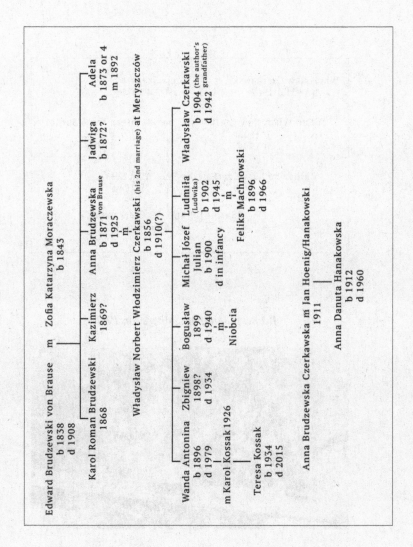

Edward Brudzewski von Brause m Zofia Katarzyna Moraczewska
b 1838   b 1843
d 1908

Karol Roman Brudzewski   Kazimierz   Anna Brudzewska   Jadwiga   Adela
1868   1869?   b 1871 von Brause b 1872?   b 1873 or 4
                                     d 1925   m 1892
                                       m
                    Władysław Norbert Włodzimierz Czerkawski (his 2nd marriage) at Meryszczów
                                     b 1856
                                     d 1910(?)

Wanda Antonina   Zbigniew   Bogusław   Michał Józef   Ludmiła   Władysław Czerkawski
b 1896   1898?   1899   Julian   (Ludwika)   b 1904 (the author's
d 1979   d 1934   d 1940   b 1900   b 1902   d 1942 grandfather)
                              m   d in infancy   d 1945
m Karol Kossak 1926   Niobcia   m
                                                     Feliks Machnowski
Teresa Kossak   b 1896
b 1934   d 1966
d 2015

Anna Brudzewska Czerkawska m Jan Hoenig/Hanakowski
                          1911

            Anna Danuta Hanakowska
                    b 1912
                    d 1960

Family Tree: Three

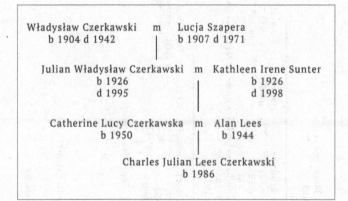

Władysław Czerkawski   m   Lucja Szapera
b 1904 d 1942   b 1907 d 1971

Julian Władysław Czerkawski   m   Kathleen Irene Sunter
b 1926   b 1926
d 1995   d 1998

Catherine Lucy Czerkawska   m   Alan Lees
b 1950   b 1944

Charles Julian Lees Czerkawski
b 1986

Below: Julian in his father's car, 1931.

A Brief Note on Polish Pronunciation

For those English speaking readers, the majority I suspect, who are daunted by Polish pronunciation, these notes are to give you some idea of the pronunciation of the names of the principle people and places in this book. Having had a lifetime of teaching people how to pronounce my surname, I understand the difficulties.

Although native speakers will quibble about exact pronunciations, here's a very short guide.

cz is *ch*

dz is *j,* as in *jive*

w is *v*

j is *y*

gn is *neu,* like the sound at the beginning of the word *neutral.*

ż with a dot over is *zh,* as in *Zhivago,* but the ordinary **z** is the same as in English albeit a little softer. So *Zbigniew* is *Zbiniev.*

Ł (L or l with a squiggle) is *w*

The stress is on the last but one syllable. This means, for example, that **Władysław** becomes *Vwadiswav,* with the stress on the 'i'

Bogusław is *Boguswav*

Dziedziłow is *Jiejiwuv*

Meryszczów is *Merishchuv*
Wanda is *Vanda*
Czerkawski is *Cher-kav-ski*

As a general rule, male surnames end in 'i' and female in 'a', so I am Czerkawska whereas my father was Czerkawski, a distinction I have preserved.

My father always used to point out to English speakers, horrified by the sight of **szcz** words, that they never have any trouble saying *push-chair*, which more or less uses the same sound.

CHAPTER ONE

A Little Boy, Weeping

As I write this, Russian troops are waging a deadly and unprovoked war in Ukraine, targeting civilians as well as soldiers. Sometimes, it seems as though they are primarily targeting civilians. The stories of atrocities, rape and looting the dead are horrific. I watch every news programme with a sickening sense of identification with and sadness for the people there, even though I myself, like most people in Britain, have never experienced the terrible reality of occupation. The difference is that I have heard about it from my father and from other older friends and relatives who experienced it, sometimes repeatedly, although all of them were reluctant to go into any kind of detail. The trauma of it, seldom if ever mentioned during my happiest of childhoods, was there, a subterranean stream of loss and sorrow, that occasionally surfaced when least expected. My father was wise, kindly, loving. But I'm glad he's not here to see Putin's war and all of the hideous parallels with what went before. For anyone who knows even a little of the tragic history of this region, it is a recurrent nightmare, a problem for which there is never a settled solution, or not, at least, while elderly dictators with dreams of empire and fears of their own mortality are able to indulge their fantasies.

It was the short video of the little boy that made me cry. There he was, walking towards the border. He had on a good warm jacket, a jacket that looked new. Bought for winter, probably. He had his little backpack, the kind kids take to school. He was carrying something in his hand, a passport I later learned. He was trudging along with dogged persistence, an exhausted little boy who knew that he had to keep going because there were monsters behind him. And he was crying his eyes out. Real, terrible, anguished tears. It haunted me. I kept thinking of all the children who had been going to school, playing games, enjoying the ordinary pursuits of childhood in ordinary homes, looking forward to spring. Everyday life, precious and mundane. Now I think of how many of them didn't survive and how many will still be sacrificed. That particular little lad made it to safety with the help of a great many people along the way, and was, I believe, reunited with his siblings. But there was another reason why it gave me such a sense of helplessness. For many years past, I've been researching and writing about my own family's sad history in Eastern Europe. And there too were stories of displacement, unspeakable cruelties inflicted on the innocent at the behest of evil men. The fact that many such evil men – but not all – face a terrible reckoning is no comfort at present, just as it was no comfort for my relatives back then.

There was a parallel that came to me immediately. In September 1939, Germany and Russia seemed set to carve up Poland between them, with Russia threatening yet again to occupy Lwów (now Ukrainian Lviv) and significant parts of the area of southern Poland and South-east Ukraine that was then called Galicia, not to be confused with the Galicia of North West Spain. This region was historically part of Poland and had been for hundreds of years. My thirteen year old father, Julian, was in Lwów with his mother, Łucja. After a great deal of agonising in the face of horrors on all sides, she sent him south with his uncle to a town called Czortków (now Chortkiv) within easy travelling distance of the border between Poland and Romania. They would cross into Romania, before travelling to Hungary, where they hoped to meet up with my grandfather, Władysław. He had been delayed elsewhere but after some hesitation Łucja decided that thirteen year old Julian should head for the border immediately. As has proved the case for many Ukrainian women and children, even that small delay was to prove disastrous.

The plan was that once Julian was safely over the border with his uncle and aunt, they would either wait there until his father could join them, or try to get to neighbouring Hungary, before moving on. Hungary, increasingly relying on trade with Fascist Italy and Nazi Germany, was no place for a Pole to stay at this time but was deemed marginally safer than Galicia. As people who had been designated 'Polish landowners' they faced immediate Soviet imprisonment for the crime of being part of 'the elite' (a catch-all term for a broad cross section of society) and deportation to the Gulags, but as a family with military training, they and their dependents would also face Nazi arrest. They figured that it might still be possible to pass through to a safer country from which they might regroup and fight. The sense of impending chaos must have been horrible and I was vividly reminded of my father's story only a few weeks ago, listening to a young British man, with a Ukrainian wife and child, describing how they were driving along the small back roads in an effort to reach the Carpathian Mountains.

Given that there was so much personal upheaval in the family at this time, I think Łucja's preference was to stay in her beloved Lwów and hope for the best. Still she was prepared to send young Julian away to safety with his uncle and aunt, with some vague notion that her son and his father, Władysław Czerkawski, might meet up and manage to get to England, from where fighting for his country might be more feasible for Władysław. The family had always been anglophiles, my grandfather spoke some English and had taught it to his son. It's very difficult for us, even now, to imagine the terrible uncertainty of that time, where one wrong decision could make all the difference between life and death, although many people in present day Ukraine are faced with the same dreadful dilemma. It is always hard to imagine in advance that any decision could or would be a matter of life and death. Surely it won't be as bad as all that, we say to ourselves. Surely if we keep our heads down, we'll be fine. The family had experienced upheaval before and survived. So Łucja stayed in Lwów, not wanting to leave her apartment and her sister behind, while her husband was elsewhere, making arrangements for a great many people who relied on him for their livelihoods, and no doubt realising whatever cash he could.

In early autumn of 1939, after a very fine summer, like a last farewell to normality, my thirteen year old father travelled south with his uncle and aunt, hoping to meet up with his father as soon as possible. These were men who knew how to fight and indeed had fought the Russians when they were younger, barely out of childhood. But on this occasion, beset by Russians on one side and Nazis on the other, their first priority was security for vulnerable family and others who depended on them. They had a good idea what was coming, and that fighting would be necessary, but you have to be a free man to fight a war. On this occasion, they had been in Czortków for only two days when the Russians marched in and closed the border. His uncle and aunt decided to stay in Czortków a little longer in case they could find some way through, but young Julian, perhaps with more foresight than his elders, insisted on going back to his mother in Lwów, worried about what would become of her. Then as now, the Russian soldiers had a reputation for extremes of brutality. Rape was just another means of subjugating the population.

Late in 1939, with Lwów now firmly under Russian occupation, he found himself on a very slow train back to the city, but it took him seven days to travel two hundred kilometres, and when he did arrive, he was so infested with fleas and lice that his mother made him undress on the doorstep and then burnt all his clothes. Nevertheless, she was very relieved to see him. And he was relieved that she was still in possession of their apartment. Who knows what tale she had told the occupying authorities, pretending that she was not married to a Polish landowner, a status that would have meant instant imprisonment and deportation to the East. It was my father I thought about, when I saw that little boy, trudging and weeping. Only two years older. The horrible reality of those experiences that sharpen the perceptions of us for whom they were part of our personal family history in so many heart-breaking ways. Worse, more recent news has shown us a three month old baby and her glowing young mother, just at that first laughing stage that all parents know, the chuckling over small things, the happiness of such small things. Mother and daughter, both dead, when Putin's army bombed their apartment block. There can be no forgiveness for such barbarities or if there is, it is only within the gift of the victims. Again, I find myself thinking about my father, who lost so much and yet was the least bitter of men. How did he do it? I think perhaps he took a decision not to let it ruin his life. To value what he had, from that time onwards. He would not allow evil men to poison his life with hatred. His triumph was in being able to achieve just that.

Years ago, friends would ask my father why he didn't go back to Poland after the war. Now they ask me the same question. What about the property abandoned there? Would there be any chance of reclaiming it? Even before Putin's war, it was difficult to explain to friends that such an undertaking would be not just fraught with danger but certainly doomed to failure. To say that Poland and Ukraine have had a troubled history would be an understatement, but also that part of Poland where my father and his family lived is now Western Ukraine, not Poland at all. As I reflected on this fact a few weeks ago, a journalist reminded me patronisingly that homes were of little importance where lives were concerned, shockingly unaware, given his profession, that in parallel with the loss of homes ran the torture and deaths of millions, in war, in concentration camps, in prison, of famine and of epidemic disease. Not just whole families, but whole communities were wiped out. Of course homes were of less importance than people but for those prepared to seize homes and imprison their occupants as traitors, life is cheap, expendable, of no consequence at all.

Current horrific news reports may give people some inkling that this part of the world has been disputed territory for a thousand years and more. Now a fiercely independent Ukraine, with desirable resources, is again fighting for the right to exist as a democratic society. These borderlands were and remain precarious places where peace or even rudimentary stability is hard won and always seems temporary. Most properties in what was then Eastern Poland were not so much abandoned as suddenly and irretrievably lost, caught between two forces that were then in collaboration, and that consequently swept all before them. I grew up with this knowledge, aware of it without knowing the details. The Iron Curtain was a reality for me. As a child, I saw it in my mind's eye as a literal curtain made of shiny metal, sweeping across Europe. Anything beyond it was an unknown land, as strange and incomprehensible as a place in a fairy-tale. There might as well have been dragons and sea monsters on the maps, as the ancient cartographers used to illustrate dangerous and unexplored territories. And now, as I write this, Russia has a leader who seems intent on resurrecting that Iron Curtain all over again.

Yet for my father, these were far from unexplored places. This was his treasured home, from which he retained precious memories of a way of life that was long gone. In

Housman's words, a land of lost content. I was well into adulthood before I understood about the 'air that kills' and the 'lost content' that no matter how happy our present, we can never quite recover. It has taken me half a lifetime to discover the nature of that far country, and to get to know something of the people who once lived there, the family that war took from me, as well as from my father.

This book is a labour of love, one I have been researching for many years, a story that in one form or another has haunted me throughout my life. There were so many questions. So much that seemed opaque, difficult. But chief among them was, what happened to the grandfather I never met, a young man who disappeared into the East, long before I was born? Who was he? Would I have loved him as I loved my Yorkshire grandfather? Would he have loved me? For much of my life those questions remained not just unanswered but unanswerable. That iron curtain made all enquiry difficult, although not impossible, as I realised once I began to research it in earnest. All the same, for most of my childhood, nobody in the family knew what had become of Władysław Czerkawski. I used to fantasise that one day, there would come a ring at the doorbell and there he would be. My Polish grandfather. It was a thought at once tantalising and frightening.

When I was born in Leeds, my refugee father was working in a textile mill by day and studying in the evenings. At the same time, he was trying desperately to improve his English. If my mother had been Polish too, we would probably have spoken that language at home, and my Polish would be better than the rudimentary shopping and ordering-in-restaurants skill I now possess. I've lived and worked in Poland and have coped there, albeit with difficulty, made all the harder because I was teaching English and as every EFL teacher knows, everyone wants to practise their English. This included one never-to-be forgotten occasion on a stormy Baltic crossing between Poland and Finland, when I was convinced that we were going to the bottom, and was so seasick that I wished we would, when my Polish cabin companion insisted (between our mutual vomiting) on asking me difficult questions about English grammar. Now, Google Translate and some helpful Polish friends have made things considerably easier.

Fortunately, before my father died, far too young, at the age of sixty-eight, I asked him to write down as much about his childhood and youth as he could remember, and he willingly complied, including making sketches and plans of the places where he had lived. Fortunately too, I had generous help from kind strangers and family members, including my grandfather's elder sister Wanda and her husband Karol Kossak, whom I visited in Poland when I was in my twenties. I had hoarded various documents and a few photographs for many years. For a long time, they were stored in a big box under our bed. I would come back to them from time to time. They inspired me to write poems and plays for radio and for the stage, and even a novel called The Amber Heart, with a Polish historical setting. Then, back in March 2020 when Covid and lockdown struck, I started to work on this material in real earnest, intent on recreating, as far as I possibly could, that time and place, not as fiction but as a true story.

Had I known what would happen in Ukraine before very long, I wonder if I would have carried on with the project? Well, maybe. But although its relevance has become indisputable, it has also become a weight on my shoulders, something I would rather not have to detail, given that history seems to be repeating itself. The sheer quantity of paperwork that I had accumulated, much of it hand-written, was staggering. I spent several weeks wrestling with it, mulling over precious documents, wondering exactly what I wanted to write and how I might be able to do it. Before I could even begin to write, I constructed a family chronology as far as I could, wrote it out on large pieces of drawing paper, and pinned it up all around my office. Most of these had to be rewritten as I discovered new dates and facts, thanks to some of the helpful people mentioned at the end of this book. I printed out the handful of family photographs I had and put them up on the old wooden filing cabinet that sits alongside my desk, so that I could occasionally glance at the people I would be writing about. I found, to my excitement, that a book written by my father's cousin, Teresa Kossak, contained a snapshot of the Czerkawski siblings from 1926. They were not named, but I managed to tease out who they were and there was my grandfather, with my grandmother Łucja, folding her hands over the slight bump that was my father, who would be born later that year.

It helped that I had already written a similar piece of non-fiction about certain tragic events in my mother's Irish family (*A Proper Person to be Detained*), and had learned about the problems and pitfalls of managing such quantities of material and turning it into something more entertaining and involving than a chronology, but I was still looking for a way into the story at the heart of it. Throughout all this time, I kept coming back to my grandfather, one of the last of the Polish horsemen or 'lancers' from an ancient cavalry family. I soon decided that I must frame my story around him and his milieu, not focusing solely on him, but trying to find out who he was, before his life was interrupted by invasion, occupation and war. Among other things, I wanted to explore the relationship between the grandfather I never knew but longed to meet, and my own father, Julian. Oddly enough, although I thought I had pinned up my photographs randomly, my grandfather is central there too, and as I glance over now, I can see him gazing back at me.

This is the result of that exploration, a journey into my family's past in a part of the world that is once again suffering because of intractable neighbours, an attempt to shed light on a story that throughout most of my life seemed to have been obscured by time, distance, imposed borders and misunderstandings. I think what has gradually emerged is as rich and strange as any tale I could invent in my fiction. At every twist and turn, at every new revelation, I came across narratives that would, all by themselves, have provided sufficient material for a book. I was moved, intrigued, and above all captivated by the richness of the narrative that was revealed. It seemed to me like finding some ancient canvas, masked by years of smoke and grime. When I began to clean it, carefully, a bit at a time, I found myself marvelling at every new detail that emerged, until eventually the whole picture shone through and – more than once – reduced me to tears.

CHAPTER TWO

Closest Family to Nobody

As the war in Europe drew to its messy and difficult end, my father, still only nineteen or twenty, found himself in Italy, in a tank division. I have his tunic badge with its splendid tank. He was there until 1946, after which he, along with many other displaced Poles, was transported to Britain, housed at Duncombe Park, near Helmsley in Yorkshire, one of many British resettlement camps, and eventually demobilised there. Because he could already speak some English, he would write love letters for his pals so that they could romance the Yorkshire girls they met at dances in the village hall. There is a certain irony about the fact that the son and heir of one of the last of the great Polish Lancers, horsemen born and bred, should find himself driving a tank.

I have copies of my father's old army documents that were useful when I came to apply to have my Polish citizenship reinstated. There is, among these documents, some record of his having been in a German labour camp after his capture in Warsaw, and a brief reference to him working in the infirmary of that camp. There was no reference at all to something that I knew to be true: his time with the Home Army. This is hardly surprising, given what happened to some of those who went back to Poland, or those who had remained there, especially in the East, under Stalinist and

Polish communist rule. Imprisonment and exile were the least of it for those who had shown themselves to be traitors to the Soviet system by supporting an independent Polish state. Serving in 'General Anders' Army', the informal name for what was originally the Polish Armed Forces in the East, was grudgingly excused by Stalin, after he had changed sides. But membership of the Polish Resistance in the form of the Polish Home Army was not forgiven, nor was fraternising with the West. I know of at least one family member who had worked in the American Embassy as a translator before the war, and was imprisoned afterwards as a western spy. For a while, my father must have agonised over whether to go back or not. He must have wondered who, if any, among his family might still be alive. And what his life might be like if he did go back, given that the places he loved and called home were no longer even in Poland.

Given the circumstances, he elected to stay.

At first, Julian lived in rather grim lodgings in Leeds and worked in a woollen mill as a textile presser. He went dancing with his fellow Poles, and on one never forgotten (or forgiven) occasion, two of them missed the last bus back to their lodgings and were turned away from a Salvation Army hostel by a warden who was deeply suspicious of foreigners. Aliens, as they were called. He met my Leeds Irish mother, Kathleen, in the Mecca Ballroom in the city centre. She was a pretty girl just a few months younger than he was. On that particular night, she had been persuaded to go dancing by her elder sisters, Vera and Nora. Her hair was tied back with a shoelace and she had a cold sore on her lip. Julian still spotted her and danced with her. It was obviously a match made in heaven. They married in 1948 and lived in a tiny two-roomed flat next to my Yorkshire grandparents' house, in the industrial heart of Leeds. He studied at night school, determinedly cycling there after work, winter and summer alike, free classes being one of the unsung post-war benefits, and they both coped with a certain amount of xenophobia, which my Irish grandmother understood all too well. All incomers recognise it.

Eventually, he gained his BSc at Leeds University. He was initially working in the department of medicine there, in geriatrics, but he found it too distressing. It's only now, when I realise what he must have gone through as a boy and young man during those pre-war and wartime years, that I fully understood why. So much of what he was dealing with must have triggered something very like PTSD, although it had no name then. People were just expected to pull themselves together and get on with life. I remember one occasion, when he had taken me into town and had fallen ill on the way back. With hindsight, I think something – I have no idea what – had triggered hideous memories for him. He was so pale that his face looked grey, and his teeth were chattering. I don't know what it was that had so upset him, but I remember, young as I was, being aware of his distress and distressed by it in turn, even though he was making valiant efforts to hide it from me. I remember my mother's mild irritation on my behalf, worried that I had been frightened. I hadn't. Only concerned. But she came from a family where you sank or swam, and that was that. Of course she changed and mellowed as she understood more, over the long and happy years of their marriage, as more emerged about the wartime experiences of the Polish people. He recovered, but he had occasional episodes of inexplicable ill health for years, until they faded altogether. In his final illness, I'm sure that some of those buried feelings and experiences came back to haunt him, but for most of his life, he was calm and contented.

One factor in this recovery was that when he was research-ing for his PhD, he transferred from human to animal biochemistry, specialising in animal nutrition and dairying. He would eventually become a recognised expert in his field. During the last few years of his working life, he travelled the world, advising developing countries on projects aimed at easing both human and animal health. It also helped him to come to terms with his wartime experiences when we moved away from the city, to a town in Scotland, from which he could divide his time between his research, his family, his beloved garden and his equally beloved countryside.

In the 1960s, he became a naturalised British citizen, but as a scientist, he was advised that he should relinquish his Polish citizenship, since Poland was still firmly behind that iron curtain. He might have to travel to conferences, and his passport wouldn't protect him, or indeed any of his family, should the country of his birth decide to keep him. It's not widely known and it certainly isn't the case now, but at that time, if a woman married a Pole, she took on his nationality, as did any children of the marriage. In the very early post war years, that even meant relin-quishing her own nationality altogether, although as Neal Ascherson so graphically illustrates in his novel The Death of the Fronsac, many British women married Poles and were then not just persuaded, but actively encouraged, to go back to Poland with them, to the Soviet Paradise, only to find that it was something less than heavenly. By then, of course, they were trapped. Britain had a swift change of heart and laws, and there are tales of British diplomats in Poland, desperately issuing British passports to women trapped in situations they hadn't anticipated. Would that happen now? Looking at the struggles of British citizens with Ukrainian wives and children, trying to bring them to the UK on spousal visas, I very much doubt it.

For all that people will now tell me how much they liked the Poles, there was a strong movement to 'send them home'. The trouble was that my father, like so many others, didn't have a home to go to. And had no idea what had become of his family. One of my saddest discoveries, when I looked closely at some of the paperwork associated with his transfer to the UK and subsequent demobilisation, was that under the heading 'next of kin' he had written in his round, still youthful hand, a Polish phrase that literally translates as 'closest family to nobody'. At that time, as far as he was aware, he had nobody. There were his army friends. I have some snapshots of groups of young men in uniform from that time, mostly from Italy. Later, there would have been friends from the resettlement camp, for whom he wrote those love letters. There would have been the handful of people with whom he shared digs in Leeds, where his first job was one of the compulsory 'reserved occupations' in a textile mill. But as far as he knew, he had nobody and nothing else except a handful of photographs and a tiny silver mirror that had belonged to his mother or his grandmother. There was certainly nowhere at all to call home.

Some Poles decided to return to Poland, only to find themselves under suspicion as western spies, especially those who had been members of the Home Army. This too explains why my father, no fool, kept very quiet about his time in the Resistance to all but myself, when he was writing his account of that time. I knew that he had been in the Warsaw Uprising. It was where he was taken prisoner by the Nazis. He had been wounded and captured. He was taken by train to Berlin, and thence via Prague, to a forced labour camp at Regensburg. He was eventually liberated by the Americans in 1945, whereupon he joined the greatly expanded General Anders' Army, in the Polish II Corps.

In 1941, after Germany invaded the Soviet Union, Stalin had suddenly found it expedient to look for allies. Or if not allies, then more cannon fodder. He therefore released tens of thousands of Polish prisoners-of-war held in Soviet camps, granted them an amnesty of sorts, (although for what crime it would be hard to say), and agreed that they could form a military force under the control of the Polish government in exile, a force which would become known as General Anders' Army. Later, new units were added to this Polish army, mainly composed of the many thousands of freed prisoners of war from German Labour Camps, Dad among them. There were also some Poles who had been forcibly conscripted into the Wehrmacht. Throughout all this time, and for long after, nobody, least of all my father, knew what had become of my grandfather, although he too had been part of General Anders' Army for a while. My father, my grandfather and his brother-in-law Feliks Machnowski, were all, at different times, part of this army. None of them were aware of this, nor did any of them know what had become of the other two, and until the day he died, my father believed that his Uncle Feliks had been killed at Katyn. In fact, he survived, was sent to a Gulag and was eventually released under Stalin's amnesty.

The Polish Government in Exile hadn't wanted the Polish refugees to go back at all, branding them traitors for submitting to Stalin's rule. Given that in the early post-war years, Stalin and his minions set up over two hundred concentration camps in Poland for Polish civilians, they were right in advising people not to go back, albeit less than charitable when it came to accusations of treachery. To add insult to injury, the Soviets also used existing camps from the Nazi occupation. Partisans who had fought the Nazis were forced to fight the Soviets all over again. It is still hard for people who have never known occupation to comprehend the day to day realities of it all. Even in 1978, when I was working in Wrocław, we were expressly warned not to discuss politics in our classes. There would, we were told, be a KGB plant in just about every classroom. As a foreign lecturer, I realised that my phone was tapped so overtly, albeit ineptly, that one evening, as I was making a call to a friend in Scotland, the crackles on the line resolved into a young male voice saying 'Good evening, English girl!'

As the Warsaw Institute so succinctly puts it, 'While Western societies went on to rebuild their homelands after the war ... gunshots were still being heard in Poland. The struggle for its independence was far from over. The Soviets had established their military bases. And through imposed terror they exerted total control over Poland, its economy, politics and society.' Control was absolute, although as time went by, the Poles not only rebuilt their beloved Warsaw from the ground up, but found ever more resourceful ways of behaving subversively, using all means at their disposal including art, religion, theatre and literature. They would joke that the best view in Warsaw was from the top of the Palace of Culture, (a massive and domineering Soviet edifice, gifted to Poland by Russia whether they wanted it or not), because it was the only place in the city from which you couldn't see the Palace of Culture.

No wonder my father decided to stay in the UK and was content to acquire a whole new family from a background so different from his own that I think the only points of contact they had, initially, must have been his Roman Catholic upbringing and my grandfather's love for England and English language classics. Mum's family were as working class as it's possible to be, but they too loved books and reading. Their mutual love never waned throughout the years of their marriage. When I first began to research and write about my Polish background, specifically in a couple of radio plays, and a stage play for Edinburgh's Lyceum Theatre, almost every person I spoke to here in Scotland would be effusive in their praise for the Polish refugees who, like my dad, elected to stay in Britain at the end of the war.

'Lovely people. They fitted in!' they would tell me, with a slight emphasis on the word 'they'. Nobody ever had a bad word to say about them.

Back then, these were people who remembered the war, and who all, oddly enough, remembered how much they had loved the Poles. Nobody ever remembered or even remarked upon those who had told them in no uncertain terms to go back where they came from. Like the woman in Leeds who asked my mum if she thought 'they should send all those Poles home?' to which my forthright mother responded that seeing as she had just married one, she didn't think it was a good idea at all. But even I didn't realise until quite recently, when I read Neal Ascherson's *The Death of the Fronsac*, that there had, to quote one shocking example, 'been a packed out rally in the Usher Hall in Edinburgh, where a church minister had been cheered as he abused the Poles as scroungers and Papists.'

Not all sunshine and roses, then.

Back in the '60s and '70s, those who thought the Poles were such lovely people had in their minds a whole generation of refugees who, I now realise, would have been traumatised into reticence and circumspection by their hideous wartime experiences, and so relieved to find asylum anywhere, that they had simply settled down to whatever jobs were offered, and thenceforward, kept a very low profile. They seldom, if ever, mentioned the war. In Yorkshire, where my dad was resettled, the choice of work at that time was between mills and mines. The Poles soon acquired the reputation of being hard-working, a reputation that ironically would be transformed into an undesirable quality by more recent ideologues and propagandists. All the same, many of the Polish families I encountered at school in Leeds hadn't really fitted in. Many of them hardly spoke any English. They had Polish clubs and Polish doctors, they worked alongside and social-ised almost wholly with other Poles.

We knew some of them and liked them very much, but since I had a Leeds Irish mother, there was a whole other side to my family, albeit one with a similar tendency to keep to their own cultural tribe. I remember the occa-sional visit to the Polish Club where I danced, standing on my father's feet, in my patent leather ankle strap shoes. We sometimes ate Polish food, including *pierogi* and plum dumplings, and I had a Polish traditional costume, with an embroidered waistcoat and tassels on my long socks. But my father's friendship circle was wider than that of many other Polish incomers. In retrospect, it's hard to criticise them. On the one hand, they sensed that they weren't really wanted. On the other, the home they had known was no longer in existence, a concept that even now I find hard to explain to people whenever they say 'why didn't your father go back to Poland after the war?' as they do now, more out of curiosity than xenophobia. Borders had shifted again. It was a different country and what would soon follow would be a long period of repression. If their pre-war homes still existed, they were occupied by other people. They truly were citizens of nowhere, even though they would never make the mistake of confusing state and nation. The idea of their nation existed deep inside them as I'm sure it exists deep inside all Ukrainians today.

One of my Leeds aunts had also married a Pole, Władysław Budzicki, a big, kindly man who worked at the Yorkshire Copperworks, and who embarrassed my eight year old self if I met him when I was out playing, by loudly and excitedly calling to me in Polish. 'Kasia, Katarzynka, Kasieńka, Kasiunia!' he would shout, in a sort of crescendo (or diminuendo?) of diminutives. He had an allotment that he tended assiduously, and he grew more gigantic cabbages than my aunt could ever use or even give away. He would buy me sweets, and I remember that he took me to Woodhouse Feast, the local visiting fairground, where I begged him to take me on the Speedway. I was fine, but he reeled off the roundabout looking very green about the gills.

When I think of him now, it is with a terrible pang of guilt and affection all mixed up together. He and his wife had no children. He loved me more unashamedly than I loved him. I was a shy child, I found him overwhelming, and I had not the faintest idea what his past experiences had been. Nor would he ever have wanted me to know. He was fond of a drink, which my mother's family found shocking, but then they had their own historical reasons for that aversion. He fitted in, in that he kept a low profile in the community and at work, and he slogged away for years at a filthy job. Then he was given a watch for his pains and died of cancer, soon after retirement. I suspect he had come from a rural area, and the allotment was the only place where he felt truly at home, truly comfortable.

Dad, meanwhile, added a PhD to his BSc, eventually moving to work as a biochemist in an agricultural research institute in Scotland, where his growing expertise was recognised by the even higher award of a DSc. There had been very little money to facilitate this career. Mum's family had none to spare and university was a foreign concept. As alien as my father with his jet black hair, his high cheekbones and his romantic notions of hand kissing and courtesy. My parents used to joke that they had been so poor during the first years of their marriage, living in a tiny two roomed flat with no bathroom and the only lavatory downstairs and through the back yard, that they shared a pair of pyjamas between them. I've occasionally wondered why Dad was different from so many others. Partly, he had been young when his entire life was disrupted, so maybe he had been able to adjust to the changes more easily. Partly, in marrying my mother, he had – more by good luck than good management – found a family that appreciated books and music, and a mother-in-law who, with her Irish Catholic background, appreciated something of what it was like to belong to a faintly despised minority in an industrial English city.

However, there was more to it than that. It was also that his background had given him a very strong sense of his own worth. It didn't ever make him selfish. He had seen too much suffering for that. But it did make him determined to get the best possible education, the sense that he had to do the best he could with the unexpected gift of a life when so many had lost theirs. Even so, there were times when he would sing 'Red are the poppies on Monte Cassino' or the Polish Christmas carol, *Lulajże Jezuniu*, (Hush Little Jesus) with a tear in his eye, times when his early experiences would catch up with him. I remember noticing this, dimly aware that my mother's family despised these shows of emotion, perhaps because they were too uncomfortably foreign. Alien. They seemed unaware of the horrors that lay beneath or perhaps they didn't want to look too closely.

Their own forebears, Irish people escaping famine, or lead miners from the Dales, had known their own horrors, but they were already somewhat removed from them by time and more recent experience. My mother, I'm certain, learned more as time went by. Theirs was a long and happy marriage and they never fell out of love. But during those first years, these two young people whose backgrounds could not have been more different must have been trying to negotiate a tricky route from a devastating past to an optimistic future.

Later, with our admission to the EU, and freedom of movement, that future looked even more positive. A whole new generation of young Poles came to the UK, not all of them plumbers or builders, but vets, doctors, nurses and teachers, while generations of young Brits took advantage of the ability to live, study and work in mainland Europe. We became complacent. Brexit seems, in part at least, to have been facilitated by the same jingoistic resentments of incoming foreigners, the same xenophobia that caused people to scrawl 'Go Home Poles' on walls in the post-war period, the skewed perception that it is the poor who take jobs and houses from the poor. This week came the news story of a man in London's Victoria Coach Station, being brutally beaten up for the crime of confessing that he came from Poland. And here we are.

CHAPTER THREE

Noon Ghosts

My father's favourite film was *Doctor Zhivago*. I love it too, and make a point of watching it whenever it's repeated, often at Christmas time. The scene where an ageing and ill Zhivago thinks he sees Lara walking along the street and struggles to attract her attention still affects me deeply. I used to think it was simply that Dad loved the familiarity and beauty of those flat, snowy, Eastern European landscapes, the sleigh rides, the jingling of sleigh bells and harness, all coupled with the powerfully emotional music, and I'm sure he did. They must have reminded him of home. But there was more to it than that, much more. I think he appreciated the evocation of uncertainty, the way in which families were divided, often for years or forever, the savagery of it all, the precariousness of life, the need to take what happiness you can where and while you can. There must have been something about the way in which Lara ultimately disappears, as so many disappeared, never to be seen or heard from again, that struck a chord with him. Perhaps there was also something about watching all that from the safety and security of a new life in the UK that appealed to him, but it made him sad and nostalgic at the same time.

I also thought, once I was old enough to know more about it, that my grandfather's story might be something like *Doctor Zhivago*, with an affectionate wife on the one hand and a passionate love affair, blighted by war, on the other. My youthful, romantic self was always seeking Lara and Yuri, when that wasn't the nature of the story at all. There was nothing clear cut about it. Like so many troubled relationships, it was much more messy, much more equivocal, although war, displacement and separation played a key part for all those involved.

For many years, I felt as though I knew more about the early history of my Polish family than I did about my more immediate forebears. My 'ancestral lands', such as they were, are now in Western Ukraine, in an area that was once part of the much larger Polish-Lithuanian Commonwealth. To simplify a very complicated history, after 1791 this Commonwealth was ruled by a monarch who was both King of Poland and Grand Duke of Lithuania. It was already one of the largest unions within Europe and it eventually had a multi-ethnic population of almost twelve million people, with Polish and Latin being the two official languages. There were high levels of ethnic diversity and, for its time, high levels of religious tolerance. Catholicism was still dominant, but freedom of worship had been guaranteed by the Warsaw Confederation Act of 1573. This was in sharp contrast to the situation in many other European countries at the time. The Ashkenazi Jewish people, who I number among my ancestors, steadily migrated Eastwards, from France and the Rhineland, seeking the protection of this Commonwealth. It was by no means perfect or free from prejudice, but it was considerably better than the alternative. It is this old Polish Commonwealth that so many of my Polish forebears recalled as a Golden Age, a land of lost content, one which they yearned to revive and recreate anew, however impractical that might seem. The Polish nobility were the *szlachta* and their ideology was Sarmatism, named for the hypothetical ancestors of the Poles, with Sarmatia as a semi-legendary name for ancient Poland. They believed in equality, (at least among their own *szlachta* class, if not for everyone else), the observance of a traditional way of life that invariably involved good horsemanship, and the cultivation of a peaceful existence in their ancient manor houses. They saw Latin as the perfect language for expressing their finer thoughts and took pride in what they called 'golden liberty'. Like all such movements, it began well, with high ideals, but degenerated over time into something more naïve and, in its most extreme form, more arrogant, and inflexible than the idealists would like to admit.

That nostalgia persists in some quarters to this day, and it's not hard to see the attraction of an extended period of power, wealth and national pride (although not, of course, for everyone, or even for the majority) from the perspective of a more recent, turbulent history. All empires topple in time, and after many decades of relative prosperity, the Polish Commonwealth entered a period of decline. It was eventually partitioned between its more powerful neighbours: Russia, Prussia and Austria. These states, among other ambitions, planned to restore the balance of power in a Central Europe that was under persistent threat from the Ottoman Empire in the East.

After a certain amount of jostling for position between these three powerful and not notably friendly neighbours, the part of Poland known as Galicia became a Polish crown land within the dual monarchy of Austria-Hungary. The name Galicia is a Latin form of the Slavic name Halych. This ancient region covered an area that today is roughly divided between South-eastern Poland and western Ukraine. This fact alone helps to explain some of the Polish response to Putin's war. The sense of a shared history, a shared heritage and, perhaps more than anything else, a shared enemy, is so recent as to remain raw, a wound that has never quite healed. The heart of historic Galicia, the place where my grandfather was born, consisted of the cities of Lwów, Tarnopol and Iwano Frankowsk, all with a Polish and Ukrainian heritage, together with their surrounding regions, towns and villages, in what is now the western part of Western Ukraine. From 1849 till 1918, the borders of Galicia remained relatively stable, although the 1914-18 war saw Poland and Ukraine again caught between Russia and Germany. My father, when asked where he came from, would often use the Austrian name of Lemberg for Lwów, the closest city to the rural estate where he was born and spent his early childhood. After the Polish Bolshevik War of 1919, the city resumed its Polish identity, but was again occupied by Russian and then German forces during WWII. The Soviets annexed the area in the post-war carve up between the three Allied powers, until Ukraine declared independence in 1991, an independence that is now under severe threat from its neighbour all over again. The West as a whole needs to understand that the latest incursion, like so many others, with all their attendant brutalities, will never be accepted or forgiven. It is not new. It involves one side digging up an imperfectly buried hatchet and using it to cut down large numbers of vulnerable people in an unprovoked attack on a sovereign nation.

Now, the place names are changed, but they are not so very different from those old Polish names, and the ghosts of a linguistic and cultural past linger on in Lviv, Ternopil and Ivano Frankivsk. Polish Lwów had once been Leopolis: the city of lions, and the lion has been a symbol of the city for centuries. It is full of lions: on pedestals, sculptures, balconies, entrances, door handles, weathervanes and bench ends, in stone, bronze, marble and cast-iron. Even the coat of arms features a vivid golden lion beneath a city gate in a blue field. This was simplified during the Soviet era, but restored to something closer to its original design after Ukrainian independence. Films and photographs of old Lwów show a fine, historic city, sure of its Polish identity back then, but one that bore some striking resemblances to Vienna, not least in its café culture, its restaurants and theatres. Its devotion to music included everything from opera and operetta to the characteristically Polish tango music that was all the rage in the 1920s and 30s of my grandparents' youth and my father's childhood.

Even during the existence of the Polish Commonwealth, the Ukrainian people, with a long and fascinating history and language of their own, knew turbulent times. With the establishment of the Commonwealth, the old Ruthenian, as the Ukrainians were called, Orthodox nobility often converted to Catholicism and they soon became indistinguishable from the Polish *szlachta*, or landed gentry. By 1596, the Greek Catholic or Uniate Church was established in Galicia alongside Roman Catholicism. This meant that the Ruthenian peasantry and small farmers sometimes turned to the devoutly Orthodox Cossacks, skilled horsemen and women and fierce fighters, for protection. But this is again to over-simplify a history of astonishing complexity. Safe to say that this area has, for many years, been marked by a fluctu-ating but persistent cultural trend towards nationalism and independence among the Ruthenian intelligentsia who went on to inspire the poorer farm workers and city dwellers. This nationalism is increasingly defined as civic nationalism. If Poles never confuse state and nation, and they don't, neither do Ukrainians, nor will they in the future, whatever its hos-tile neighbour asserts.

By the time my grandfather, Władysław Czerkawski, was born in 1904, Galicia had a mixed population of Poles, Ruthenes and Jewish people. Although, on the whole, the Poles owned the land and the Ukrainian and Jewish people worked on it, sometimes mutinously, there had been a great deal of intermarriage, as is the case with all dis-puted territories. Again on the whole, Poles were Roman Catholic and Ukrainians were Russian or Greek Orthodox, but there was very little religious animosity between them, even when there was social unrest and prejudice. There was certainly antisemitism, although there too intermar-riage had played a part. Although divisions had flared in unspeakable ways, they had also been tempered by time, human nature and an inclination towards acceptance on a personal level, so that I number Orthodox priests and Ashkenazi Jews among my Czerkawski forebears. My grandfather and great grandfather were on friendly terms with the local Orthodox priest, and frequently attended his services, even though their children were baptised in the Roman Catholic church.

The thread of my grandfather's life and death in the faraway place that was the mysterious background to my childhood runs through this narrative. To tell this tale, I found myself navigating the uncertain seas of family history: facts about relationships that people everywhere try to pin down with tables and trees, with dates and with assumptions that are, inevitably it seems, challenged by new discoveries. Lies are told more often than you might believe. More than once, I have realised that the reasons behind those lies can be more illuminating than the truth. People do and say what they must to survive. Unpleasant facts are fudged. Motivations are misunderstood. Most of all, people tend to oversimplify intractable situations, in accord with cherished beliefs, imagining how they themselves would have behaved differently, when the reality is that they would probably have behaved in exactly the same way.

The more I, and those who have been generous in helping me, go digging, the more knowledge comes to light, but also, the more questions arise. There is mystery upon mystery, as a relative remarked, perhaps because this is a story of contested lands and the destruction of people and property, where nothing was ever safe or secure, never had been, nor will be for the foreseeable future. The more I discovered, the more it struck me that much of what I was trying to learn about had been swept away by one conflict after another, one uprising after another, one changing allegiance after another, so that it was as if those who had gone before had never been: people, houses, gardens, ways of life, all gone, never to return. I was exploring in a world of ghosts. And even though travel to physical places might have been possible in normal times, these were Covid times. Now, of course, travel to these places seems more impossible than ever. Perhaps as far as this book is concerned, the land of lost content should remain elusive. It is not possible to walk those happy highways again. But a thoughtful Polish friend said to me 'the dead want to be acknowledged' and that seemed to me to be a profound and poetic statement, because they do. Those blue remembered hills were populated by real people and you don't need to see ghosts to feel as though the dead are urging you to remind others of their very existence.

A sense of misunderstanding, unfamiliarity and sometimes sheer ignorance about Eastern Europe persists, even though it is on all our news channels and the world seems a much smaller place than it once was. When I went back to researching this book, years after my father's death, I had hardly anyone to talk to about these issues, with the exception of a few good Polish friends here in Scotland and elsewhere, and one or two knowledgeable historians. Instead, I was faced with a string of challenging questions. Why didn't your father go back home? Why didn't he manage to get in touch with his mother until fifteen years after the end of the war? How could that happen? Why did all the borders change? And perhaps even more extraordinary than that: was your father a prisoner-of-war over here?

Even for much older British people now, their only memory of the war is a hazy childhood impression of

returning soldiers and ration cards. People who experienced the war at first hand were, on the whole, reluctant
to talk about it. People whose knowledge comes mainly
from film, television and books are inclined to evoke it in
heroic terms more frequently than seems wise. Ignorance
is forgivable, because even for me, this is a story of things
I thought I understood and found I didn't. There were a
myriad of small details that crept up on me and then quite
suddenly overthrew my understanding of a past that seems
to me to be as fluid and changeable as the ocean. Or, more
appropriately, as a field of grain on a windy day. Because
this is also the story of a country childhood, of several
rural childhoods, in which the ominous *Południca*, a noon
ghost, always a woman, may come walking through the
fields towards you in the drowsy heat of the day, moving
in a cloud of dust, a scythe or a pair of shears in her
hand. She'll stop you and ask you impossible questions.
If you can't answer her, she may drive you mad, or even,
in extreme cases, cut off your head with her scythe. Well,
there have been times, I'll admit, especially when I encountered the prisoner-of-war question, when I wished I had a
handy scythe. But if I, for whom it is part of my heritage,
find all this difficult to comprehend, how much more difficult must it be for somebody born and bred elsewhere,
subject to the vagaries of uninformed commentary about
it, not least right now when every news channel struggles
to comprehend the incomprehensible.

For some older British people in particular, Eastern
Europe still feels very far away, a haunt of dragons,
whereas for many younger people, the whole continent is

their home. Now, suddenly, that region and its people are thrown into sharp relief. The ignorance of most in the west is also thrown into sharp relief. The term 'westsplaining' – the west attempting to explain our own history to us, often with a little sneer at our simplicity – is a sharp reminder of what we have to contend with. This is, above all, a story of lives and loves interrupted as they are currently being interrupted all over again. Which perhaps explains my need to illuminate them and to try to answer my own questions, at the risk of being overwhelmed by the sorrow of it all.

CHAPTER FOUR

WARNING: Poland

For many years, we did not talk about my father's home. I think this was his choice, as much as my English and Irish family's choice. It never seemed to occur to them to ask. I have Polish second and third generation friends who had the same experience, and now, older and wiser, they wish they had asked more, pressed for more information, because their parents and grandparents were largely silent. Partly, it may have been a form of survivor's guilt. Partly, these people felt embarrassed about their own nostalgia, in the certain knowledge that nobody in their new country could understand the reality of what had happened to them. We know now that the experiences of young soldiers fighting in the trenches of WW1 were utterly incomprehensible to those at home, but the grim realities of occupation even now seem beyond the grasp of many British and US citizens. I think it was one reason, among many, why Polish refugees in the UK tended to stick together. I had the advantage that as a playwright and novelist, I had already asked my father to write down an account of his past and he had complied. Even so, I find myself wishing he were here right now, so that I could talk to him again, discuss, clarify. Most of all, I want to ask him more about my grandfather, a man whose family and world collapsed about his ears as finally and irrevocably as a burnt house.

Google Earth has been my friend, just as Google Translate has been my assistant during the past few Covid-haunted years. Many years ago, when I first started researching this book, the only map I could find of the area that my forebears had called home, was a Soviet era aeronautical map, a 'tactical pilotage chart' from 1988. I can't remember where I found it, Amazon still being only a faint gleam in Bezos's eye, but maybe I sent away for it from a specialist bookshop. It covers 'Austria, Czechoslovakia, Hungary, Poland, Romania, USSR' – a lot of ground. It is scattered with dire exclamatory admonitions such as 'WARNING. POLAND. Flying outside controlled airspace and ATS routes is PROHIBITED.' I can see the Polish border and I can see the city of Lwów (Lviv on this map) in the USSR, but the map is also dotted with tantalising 'name unknown' labels, and back then, when I looked for the places whose names I did know, because they had become a part of my own story, they were not to be found. Not then, anyway. The map is as empty and threatening as those ancient maps where if you venture over the edge of the known world, you find yourself in dangerous territory.

Cue forward some thirty years and in pandemic-induced lockdown, I can type the names, or their new spellings, into Google Maps, and not only can I see satellite images of these places, but I can hone in on them, hovering above villages. In some of them, I can even click on Street View and drift, ghost-like, along roads and among scenery that my late father would probably have recognised, so little changed does it seem, passing buses and other vehicles, like the red car with its bonnet raised, probably because of some mechanical problem, two adults and a small child waiting in the sunshine for assistance, frozen in this moment like fossils in amber, and witnessed by me a few years later. When I look at Didyliv, the Ukrainian name for the village of Dziedziłow, where my father was born, I can glide up and down the main road there, looking right and left at fields, and poplar trees, at this or that building. The thought that we may be heading back towards those blank maps covered in warning signs is chilling indeed, as is the constant speculation about what might now be happening to some of those people, ordinary souls going about their precious everyday lives.

I can immediately understand why Dad was so fond of Ayrshire, where he spent most of his adult life, because there are such similarities between these green woods and fields of Ukraine, so vivid that I can almost smell the scent of cut grass and spring blossoms, and the softly undulating Ayrshire landscape he loved and sketched in watercolours over many years. It must have felt like home to him, and when my parents moved to the town of Maybole, in South Ayrshire, his friendships with farmers must also have had a certain familiarity about them. Only a couple of years ago, one of them, a generation younger than my dad, came up to me at a meeting.

'You're Julian's daughter, aren't you?' he said. 'I still think about your dad often. He was such a good friend. A wise man.'

My father eventually became a biochemist, specialising in animal nutrition, which made it all the more moving to discover that his great grandfather had written and published extensively about agriculture and new farming methods and that his grandfather and father had taken a similar interest.

Trees in early leaf are growing along this road through Didyliv, and in the village there are buildings, both ramshackle and well kept, with the occasional person working outside. There is a shop, a bus stop with a handful of people waiting, a petrol station. There is a person wearing a red hat, standing in a patch of garden ground, watching the world go by. There's a fancy motorbike. A tall tree. Another beautiful Orthodox church. On one stretch of the main road through the village, where a tributary lane leads up between trees and meadowland, past farm buildings, there is a mysterious glimpse of horses, ten or more, possibly escaped from some farm. They are cantering dangerously along the verge at the side of the road, manes flying. Frustratingly, I can't turn up this or that side lane. I can only turn around and around at the click of a mouse, and peer into the distance. Suddenly, to the left of the road, I come across a pair of impressive lions, sturdy in creamy yellow stoneware, with wide shallow steps between them, a low wall leading back on either side, and a few mature trees, including a massive weeping willow, surrounding them, like the remains of parkland. Beside them, an oblivious man in a red shirt is smoking a cigarette. They are marking, surely, the entrance to the old estate that my grandfather inherited from his great uncle Julian, a politician and a medical doctor, who had lived there for many years. This can't have been a carriageway, since there are steps, but it looks like an important entrance all the same.

Now they seem to mark the entrance to nothing but an open meadow. You can see a small herd of brown and white cows, much like traditional Ayrshires, grazing or chewing the cud. The lions, each with front paws resting on a fallen animal, hard to identify exactly what, gaze over the road, their original purpose, like so many of the people who once lived here, obsolete, long forgotten.

There are photographs that visitors have taken over the years and posted online, pictures of the tall, semi-derelict, red brick Roman Catholic church that was built during my grandfather's time. There are several pictures of a lake, a cool blue-grey eye, fringed by reeds, and by many small trees and shrubs, the image taken in spring with that vivid early green surrounding a stretch of water. I recognise the lake from stories my father told me about it. Again, it seems very odd to be able to see it like this, even on a screen, to impose my memories of those tales upon this present day picture. Not for the first time, I want my dad to be here so that I can show him these images. I want to say 'Look, look. Here it all is. You can see it again.' But whether he would have wanted to see it again is another matter entirely, because it saddens even me, who for most of my life did not really appreciate all that was lost.

It explains why Ukrainians will carry on fighting as long as it takes.

In winter, this place is very cold, a snowy landscape where, in my grandfather's time at least, transport was much easier by sleigh. My grandfather Władysław Czerkawski wasn't born here. He was born seventy kilometres south-east of Dziedziłow, in another village, a place called Meryszczów, (now Mereshchiv) the true family home of this branch of the Czerkawskis for many hundreds of years. He was his parents' youngest son, the child of a typical Polish *szlachta* family, with a great deal of pride, but not always, or even often, with matching amounts of disposable income. The parallels with some of the Scottish 'county set' are irresistible: old names, crumbling mansions, a certain extravagance, an abiding love of the land and the endless need for ready cash.

Handsome Władysław, was born on 14th January in 1904. He was born in a sleigh. How my great grandmother, a rather delicate young woman named Anna Brudzewska, came to give birth to her sixth child in a sleigh, in January, is not a story of which I have any details. But those are the facts as related by my father whose family had told him the story, repeatedly, in the way that all family tales are repeated by uncles and aunts. She could have been on her way to a doctor or midwife, but I would imagine that for a woman of her station in life, they would certainly have come to her. More likely is that she had been visiting neighbours, and gone into labour as she was on her way home. With a sixth child, labour could have been sudden and swift. The sleigh would probably have been one of those long, flat, horse-drawn affairs, with straw bales covered by sheepskins and blankets, making it reasonably comfortable. You could lie down on them. Perhaps it had even been chosen because of her condition. Who knows? A redoubtable woman. How did she come to marry into the Czerkawski family and what happened afterwards?

CHAPTER FIVE

Korabniki

Anna Brudzewska von Brause, my great grandmother, was born in 1871 at a place called Lednogora, in what was known as Greater Poland. She was the daughter of Edward Brudzewski and Zofia Katarzyna (the Polish version of my own name, Catherine) Moraczewska. I have three, possibly four mementoes of her. One is a high-necked lace collar that my father's cousin, Teresa, gave me. Teresa's mother, Wanda, was Anna's eldest daughter, and Wanda had managed to preserve a handful of souvenirs of her mother. There is also a head and shoulders photograph of her, discovered unexpectedly in the book that Teresa wrote mainly about her father's family. She has an oval face and wide-set dark eyes. Her coiled hair is piled up on top of her head. She is gazing out at the photographer, her lips pursed. She's dressed in dark satin, a pretty woman with an other-worldly and faintly disapproving air about her. It's hard to imagine her giving birth in a sleigh. The third keepsake, which may or may not have belonged to Anna, is a Baltic amber necklace of simply threaded beads, each one containing a tiny fossil, most of them fossil seeds. Wanda herself gave this to me back in the 1970s, when I visited her and her husband, Karol Kossak, in Poland. A fourth souvenir was brought to England by my father at the end of the war: a tiny silver mirror with delicate cream enamel work on the back. It's old and precious and I think it came out of one of those nineteenth-century dressing cases that ladies and gentlemen used while travelling. I thought it had belonged to my grandmother Łucja , and that may well be true, but Łucja was a twentieth-century girl, and it has the look of something from an older world, so that too may have belonged to Anna.

In 1871, a hundred years before my first trip to Poland, Anna was born at the manor house of Lednogora. It had come into the family as part of a dowry, when Anna's mother, Zofia Moraczewska, whose family had owned it since the beginning of the nineteenth century, married Edward Brudzewski, my great grandfather. The Moraczewskis were an interesting and intellectual family. Zofia's brother was an architect and her nephew was the first Prime Minister of the Republic of Poland. By 1885, though, a bank is listed as owning the property, so the estate must have been auctioned off some time before, while Anna was a child. Nothing daunted, Edward bought himself a place called Korabniki, a very pretty manor house that is now in private ownership. It was not far from Kraków, a cultural centre, then as now. There were several children of the marriage: Karol, who became a sculptor in Kraków, Zofia, named for her mother, Kazimierz, Anna, Jadwiga and Adela, the youngest daughter.

Edward is intriguingly described as 'landowner and insurgent' which in those turbulent times was definitely complimentary. He had served in the ranks of the Prussian cavalry and as a young man had taken part in the January 1863 uprising against the Austrian authorities. Uprisings of one kind or another were a feature of life in this part of the world, as perennial as the seasons. He went into exile in France, as did so many insurrectionary and patriotic Poles, but when things settled down, he returned to Poland and there he became a friend of the much younger playwright, painter and poet Stanisław Wyspiański, born in 1869. For those who know little about Polish literature and art, which is most of the English speaking world, it would be hard to overestimate Wyspiański's standing in the Polish national consciousness and his celebrity at the time, although that didn't necessarily bring financial success in its wake, any more than it does today. Edward Brudzewski even features in one of Wyspiański's dramas, an epic play called Liberation. The friendship was genuine enough. The *szlachta* were traditionally much more keen on the arts than their hunting and shooting British counterparts.

The story of Wyspiański's life is fascinating. His patriotic dramas may not be to modern tastes, but his paintings are a different matter. His many sketches and portraits of his own children are wonderfully loving and realistic. My favourite is called *Motherhood*, now in the National Museum in Warsaw, a woman gazing down at the chubby baby she is breastfeeding. There is such tenderness in this picture. The blue of her dress, the paler blue of the child's dress, the curve of the mother's breast and the intensity of her gaze all serve to create an image that leaps off the canvas at you with the sense that the artist himself is fully engaged with mother and baby alike. He certainly was, since this is a picture of his wife and child. His wife was Teodora Pytko, a year his senior, and a one-time servant in his aunt's house. The circumstances of their first meeting are unclear, although there is a possibility that he met her when she was contemplating suicide after realising that she was pregnant with another man's child, and he himself may even have found her the position in his Aunt Joanna's house. Later, he adopted the child of this pregnancy, a son named Tadeusz, as his own.

The relationship was very much frowned upon. A social disaster. Even today, his extensive Wikipedia entry contains only one short reference to his wife: 'In 1900, Wyspiański married the mother of his four children, Teodora Pytko.' It's hard to exaggerate how shockingly it would have deviated from the Kraków conventions, excused only because of people's perception of Wyspiański as a nonconformist bohemian who couldn't be expected to behave properly. No such leeway was ever given to poor Teodora. Aunt Joanna, regretting her impulsive generosity, seems to have maintained a deep detestation of Wyspiański's wife for years, but the scathing accounts of the relationship emanating from Aunt Joanna and from the artist's own friends are one sided at best. The couple were at least acquainted from the 1890s, before and after he travelled to Paris, and remained together until his early death in 1907. It's a familiar story. This was a woman who took care of his household and his uncertain finances, while raising his children, struggling with real privation, only varied by episodes of abject poverty, all of which her husband seems unwilling to alleviate. He can't have been the easiest of men to live with. For a long time, she looked after him, mothering him, much as she mothered her children, and seeming all unaware or uncaring of his status as a national treasure. Perhaps that suited him. Perhaps it was the only way she could cope with him.

Portraits and, later, photographs of Teodora show a strong woman, with an uncompromisingly square, serious face (the artist did not flatter her) but with a beautiful and rather sensuous mouth. They had children together before they were married, in 1900, but it's clear that he himself found the discrepancy in their backgrounds difficult to come to terms with. Some have said that he married her out of pity, but pity is close kin to love, and who knows what goes on in any partnership? His circle of friends and relatives thoroughly despised her, and despised her more, the longer the marriage lasted. Even allowing for these prejudices, the couple seem to have been less than suited to each other. But something kept them together.

His own descriptions of her read like somebody attempting to justify an intense and overwhelming physical attraction while damning its object with faint praise, in an effort to excuse his own shame at exploiting her. But perhaps I'm maligning him. After the artist's decline and early death from syphilis in 1907, a cruel disease which he does not seem to have passed on to his partner, Teodora remarried, and lived bravely on through the trials of the first half of the twentieth century, until 1957.

Throughout some of this scandalous period, Wyspiański was a frequent visitor to the Brudzewski house at Korabniki, although Teodora would never have accompanied him. I doubt if she was ever invited. The original house was built in the mid fifteen hundreds, by a remote relative of a different branch of the family. It seems to have been a comfortable old manor house, surrounded by attractive gardens, and it became a favourite retreat for the artist who visited the

Brudzewski family there between 1886 and 1889. There is even the remains of a 600 year old oak tree under which legend says that the playwright would sit to write.

There may have been other attractions at Korabniki.

Wyspiański was very fond of the young Brudzewska sisters, Anna and Adela in particular, and of the two, it seems as though Adela was most susceptible to his charms, most likely to return his feelings. I suspect that great grandmother Anna was charmed by him, as so many young women were, but her affections already lay elsewhere. Wyspiański first met the sisters in Kraków, when they would have been in their teens, probably at some literary or artistic salon. They were known for their beauty, their style and intelligence and would have been welcome guests at these events. When Ludwik Tomanek, who knew the couple, writes of Teodora 'if she were any other woman, educated and worldly, who knows if Wyspiański would be so happy with her', he could have been thinking about the well-educated Brudzewska sisters, who flirted with the poet, who were entertained by him at a time when young women's lives were restricted by convention, and who missed him when he was away. Coquettishly, they wrote to him of Korabniki: 'Don't forget about us, or our happy hours spent wandering through the gardens.' They were not, in present day terms, particularly sophisticated, but they would have been educated young women, conscious of their place in the world. Education was prized for girls as well as boys.

Wyspiański was undoubtedly a good-looking young man and it's a little hard not to sympathise with Edward Brudzewski who foresaw an unhappy, not to say scandalous future for Adela with such a celebrity, given that he was already deeply entangled with Teodora, and that everyone in their circle knew it and disapproved of it. Edward was reluctant to break off his own friendship with the great artist, not just admiring the man's talent but quite simply liking him. However, he certainly sought to remove his daughters from this disruptive influence. It was something of a relief to him when Wyspiański devoted large parts of the years from 1890 to 1895 to travelling throughout Europe, most vitally to Paris, a key point in his artistic development. Certainly when Wyspiański was in France, he wrote to the family with evident nostalgia for the house and its inhabitants, saying, romantically and flatteringly, 'it is always spring at Korabniki'. The nightingales always sang there.

If it was always spring at Korabniki, Edward had autumnal ideas in mind, because in 1892 Adela was strongly encouraged – not to say forced – into a marriage with a much older friend of her father, and it's hard not to conclude that this was done to protect her from the attentions of the fascinating artist and poet who could weave magic spells with images and words alike. I've often wondered whether any of Wyspiański's paintings of unknown, fresh faced young women, of which there are many, are of the Brudzewska sisters. Surely he must have sketched them? But perhaps they went unnamed to avoid any breath of scandal.

As for Anna, she was already being courted by, as far as her father was concerned, anyway, a much more appropriate suitor: my great grandfather, Władysław Czerkawski of Meryszczów in the Eastern part of the country. She was in her early twenties, and he was around forty and in all likelihood already a widower. He was experienced and charming, with all the sophistication that time spent in Vienna could give him, but he was soft hearted and romantic too. The discrepancy in ages was not uncommon at the time, nor were second and even third marriages, since childbirth was fatal for so many women.

CHAPTER SIX

Modestly Devoted to
Dogs and Hunting

Along with the horrors of occupation, one of the most difficult things to try to explain to British friends is how often
and how dramatically borders have shifted in this part of the
world, frequently in the most deadly fashion. Like those who
make their homes on the slopes of a volcano, people knew
that the possibility of disaster was never very far away. What
we are seeing now in Ukraine is a graphic illustration, in the
most horrific way possible, of the sheer speed and intensity
with which everyday life can be turned upside down. And
yes, we know that it has been happening all over the world,
but the closer it is, human nature being what it is, the more
we are able to identify with it. Just a few days ago, I watched
blurred footage of a Russian helicopter, taking desperate eva-
sive action, before eventually being shot down somewhere
in Ukraine. The thing that struck me most vividly was the
very familiarity of the rural agricultural landscape, the froth
of white blackthorn fringing the fields, just as it is fringing
the fields here and now, in the west of Scotland. I caught
myself thinking 'there will be sloes later'. Events in Ukraine
are bound to affect us, just as most people of my age remember the Bosnian war with a peculiarly immediate sense of
horror, because we were looking at streets and shops and
cafés just like ours and were learning an object lesson about

impermanence. We may not approve of the human need to identify with people to sympathise with them more intensely, but we can't help ourselves. It's like the period immediately after childbirth when women suddenly become mother to the whole world, and can't observe cruelty to children anywhere, even in a television drama, without an overwhelming sense of raw grief.

The Czerkawskis were indisputably Polish. There's a family coat of arms. The motto is *Jelita*, roughly translated as 'guts', although I suppose we could take it to mean courage. I'm looking at it as I type this, nicely done in stained glass, a scarlet shield with three lances, the centre one pointing downwards, a ducal orb and crown and on the top, a rather engaging horned goat, rising up out of the crown: a 'demi goat, rampant, proper' as heraldry has it. While a rampant goat might not seem quite as classy as a rampant lion or unicorn, I'm very fond of my family coat of arms. It's said to be one of the oldest in Poland, and belongs to many families, not just the Czerkawskis. Other surnames allowed to bear this coat of arms include Dąbrowski, Zamoyski and Dziduski. We are the same clan.

A Polish mediaeval chronicler named Jan Długosz says that those who bear the Jelita coat of arms are 'a clan born in Poland of men who are modestly devoted to dogs and hunting.' As usual, the women are not thought worthy of mention, although they too were modestly devoted to dogs and hunting. This would have been a fair description of the vast majority of my more recent and also my ancient forebears whose stories I now know, although my late father was never devoted to hunting. He could handle a gun, but only for target shooting. He liked a spot of fishing, had once upon a time been a good horseman, and was very fond of dogs. The first depiction of the coat of arms was said to be on the seal of Tomisław z Morska in 1316. However, my father told an even older story, of a forebear who fought in the battle of 'Dog's Field', on 24th August, 1109, during the reign of King Bolesław III. Yet another story is that the coat of arms as currently constituted was established in 1331 by King Władysław Łokietek – 'Little Elbow' – after a battle against a 40,000 strong army of Teutonic Knights, a battle which was won by the Poles who allegedly, but somewhat incredibly, lost only forty soldiers.

The motto Jelita is associated with one of these battles. A man called Floryan Szary (meaning Floryan Grey) from Łódź was badly wounded in the stomach. The king was touring the battlefield, saw him and said 'How this poor brave soldier must be suffering!' whereupon the soldier, with a certain opportunism, coupled with a characteristically Polish ability to maintain a grudge on the very threshold of death, said 'This wound doesn't bother me half as much as my terrible neighbour at home.'

'Don't worry,' said the king. 'If you survive this, I'll free you from your neighbour.' Florian recovered, probably spurred on by invigorating thoughts of revenge, and the king kept his word and gave him his nasty neighbour's property to boot, although another version of the tale maintains that he was given a grant of lands in Eastern Poland from where my own branch of the family originates. Floryan seems to have had a coat of arms already, so perhaps it was this simpler version that dated from the earlier battle of Dog's Field. At any rate Floryan and his clan were nicknamed Goat Horn. I've no idea why, and chroniclers are disappointingly silent. Długosz, in relating the story, says that poor Floryan was 'slashed with many wounds' but managed to stay conscious, trying to stuff his guts back from whence they came. The king was so impressed by this insouciance that he knighted him on the spot and ordered his surgeons to take care of him. After the battle, the king added three lances to the shield on Floryan's old coat of arms including one that pointed downwards, to commemorate the wound.

There is a large gap in time between Floryan holding in his intestines and blaming his neighbour, and those members of Clan Jelita who are recognisably from the Czerkawski family, although they do seem to have originated in those endlessly disputed Eastern territories, which perhaps lends some credibility to the notion that Floryan was given land in the East. Some accounts state that the name Czerkawski originated at a place called Cherkasy on the Dnieper, in central Ukraine, a city that was eventually incorporated into the Russian Empire. Just to complicate matters there is (or was) a village or town also called Czerkasy much closer to Lwów, and it is this place that the National Library in Warsaw associates with the Czerkawski family. The only settlement I can see on a modern map that might once have been named Czerkasy, is a large village called Shchyrets, on the Shchyrka River. From the single street view, it's certainly a place with some history.

Czerkawskis, not surprisingly, pop up during various battles, including the seventeenth-century battles against the Turks. After the 1683 siege of Vienna, more Czerkawskis are given noble status because of valour in battle. That particular battle involved the defeat of the Ottomans at the very gates of Vienna, with the help of the Polish Lithuanian Commonwealth, notably the Winged Hussars of legend, the terrifying cavalrymen with their fabulous, menacing, eagle feather armour, even the noise of which, as they rushed into battle, was said to inspire fear in the hearts of their enemies.

Anna Brudzewska, in becoming engaged to Władysław Czerkawski, was marrying into a family of some distinction, albeit one that was slightly beneath her on the social scale. Better by far than a wandering poet and painter though. His father, Władysław Jan Paweł, had been Court Counsellor to the Emperor Franz Joseph in Vienna, an occupation to conjure with. Władysław, incidentally, is a family name of such ubiquity that it makes tracing histories very confusing. There is a portrait of this same older Władysław in the archives of the Austrian National Library, under the title Ladislaus von Czerkawski, with the inscription 'Hofrath' which indicates that he had been a kind of military attaché. He received a decoration in 1885 in acknowledgment of his many years of military service, and the portrait probably dates from that time: a slightly grim, but capable man with a moustache worthy of Poirot himself – Poles loved their moustaches – and the recognisable widow's peak hairline that was passed on to his descendants.

Władysław Jan Paweł, he of the fine moustache, married a young woman named Maria Walitschek from a wealthy Viennese family. Their son was born in 1856. His full name was Władysław Norbert Włodzimierz Czerkawski, and he was my great grandfather. Following a military career in

Vienna, like his father before him, he had been an Imperial Royal 2nd Lieutenant. He had a certain sophistication about him, as far as Anna was concerned, certainly enough to counter the dubious attractions of poverty stricken poets and painters like Wyspiański. Vienna is threaded through the Czerkawski story like something rich and heady, as enticing as those cakes, pancakes and dumplings: *sachertorte, apfelstrudel* and *kaiserschmarren*, giving its name to the pancake yellow colour of so many of the central European manor houses of the time.

In the early 1980s, my biochemist father worked for the International Atomic Energy Commission in Vienna for a couple of years. We visited him and my mother, and were struck, not just by how much we liked the city, but by how comfortable my father seemed to be there: relaxed and cheerful, like somebody who has unexpectedly come home after many years of absence, and is revelling in the feeling of familiarity, as I'm sure he was. It wasn't just the music, the art and the architecture he loved. It was the café culture that he must have remembered from his childhood and missed: those exciting expeditions to Lwów with his father, where they invariably visited the cafés and patisseries, and sampled the delicious cakes of the old Austro-Hungarian empire.

In spite of the Viennese connection, great grandfather Władysław's heart was firmly at his beloved family home, a rural estate called Meryszczów in Galicia. Recently, a helpful friend, Michał Zaleski, discovered a newspaper advertisement from 1900 for a plant and seed company, in which my great grandfather is one of those offering a testimonial – a review if you like. He praises the seller and confirms that he has been a customer for twenty years, bought his asparagus seedlings from them fifteen years previously, and his asparagus bed is still providing him with delicious, nicely scented vegetables. This review is signed and dated 1899, by which time he would have been married to Anna Brudzewska for a few years, but it suggests that he has called Meryszczów his home for the past 20 years at least, even though he has spent so much time in Vienna. He has certainly been caring about, if not precisely for, the estate and kitchen garden there. I note that he signs himself Władysław Jelita Czerkawski, using his family motto in the middle of his name, a habitual practice of the *szlachta*. I love the thought of him carefully tending his asparagus bed, even though I'm pretty sure that there would have been a gardener or two. Perhaps it's because I can see my own father, his grandson, doing exactly the same thing. In the small Scottish town where he lived until his premature death in 1995, he lovingly tended his fruit and vegetable garden for many years.

This was a second marriage for my great-grandfather. While he was still a young man in Vienna, he had married Fryderyka Mick (pronounced Mitsk) and they had a son called Julian, who apparently stayed on in Vienna. This man also had a military career but, given that he was their step brother, he was largely absent from the scene as far as the later Czerkawski children were concerned. My father knew nothing about this extra great uncle. Fryderyka must have died young, possibly in childbirth, so perhaps he had been brought up by her relatives in Vienna. He didn't inherit the tenancy of the family home at Meryszczów, so he may have died before his father, or perhaps he was simply too settled in Vienna to want to move to those precarious Eastern lands.

In 1885, well before his second marriage to Anna Brudzewska, we find my great grandfather Władysław, not yet thirty years old, applying for confirmation of the 'noble title' belonging to his name. When he submits the application, he includes a string of documents: the birth certificate of his grandfather Ignacy, son of Benedict, of Meryszczów, the birth certificate of Ignacy's son Władysław Jan Paweł, and his own birth certificate, as well as an extract from the impressively named Book of States of the Kingdom of Galicia and Lodomeria, in which the nobility of Benedict Czerkawski, crest Jelita, is confirmed. There's a flavour of Genesis about this and when I visited them in 1970s Poland, various members of my family were still doing it, trying hard to place me in the annals of the Czerkawskis. The confirmation of his nobility is to be sent to 4 Grodzicki Street in Lwów, and the paperwork is to be handed to one Julian Czerkawski there. This particular Julian Czerkawski was not his son, but his uncle, a medical doctor and politician, with connections both in Vienna and Lwów. He is important to this story, like the improbably wealthy uncle of fiction who leaves a stunning inheritance to an unexpected legatee.

Confirmation of the nobility of the family was clearly vital to great grandfather Władysław. He had two reasons. He had already thought about marrying into the undoubtedly posh Brudzewski family, well before he approached Anna's father to ask for her hand, and he wanted to be sure of his status. The other reason may have been that he wanted to confirm his title to Meryszczów, via his direct relationship to Benedict, given that other distinguished families had some claim to the estate through dowries and marriage settlements. The marriage between Anna Brudzewska and Władysław Norbert Włodzimierz Czerkawski of Meryszczów (as ever, Polish names are not for the faint-hearted) took place in 1895 and was undoubtedly a love match.

CHAPTER SEVEN

Nightingales and
Flea Circuses

Of all the tales of the past that have come together to make this book, the story of the nightingales has intrigued me. Anna and Władysław set up home together on the family estate called Meryszczów, south-east of Lwów. There was a small manor house, with gardens, orchards, out-buildings and a large glasshouse, all surrounded by fields where a variety of crops were grown. Maps from the 18th and 19th centuries show a house of this same shape and size with an associated village, but there was an estate on this site even before that.

When he was a boy and during his early teens, my father visited the house at Meryszczów from time to time. He had been born at Dziedziłow and spent his early childhood there, but he knew Meryszczów well. He sketched it for me, and described it as a picturesque building of old stone, plastered inside and out and painted white, close by a small river called the Gniła Lipa. It was built into a hillside so that the front entrance, with its steep sloping roof, was on the first floor. My father's cousin, Teresa Kossak, writing about her mother's memories of her family home for so many years, confirms this configuration, and notes that 'Its architecture was unusual; the house stood on a small slope, so it looked like it had only the ground floor and attic at the front, but there was another floor visible from the courtyard.'

When Dad sketched it for me from memory, he drew a short drive and turning circle. From the back, there was a central section, with a roofed turret above and small wings, extending at right angles to the main building. There was a narrow driveway edged with massive lindens, leading up to double doors, with lawns on either side. Running along the back of the house, including the two wings, was a traditional carved wooden balcony or veranda, some of it glassed in for protection in winter. This was supported on pillars, making a sort of cloister of the garden below. A photograph of the younger members of the Czerkawski family, taken early in 1926 at Meryszczów, gives us a glimpse of a sturdy stairway, with a banister rail and balustrade, leading up to this veranda. The slates on the roof were reddish brown, contrasting vividly with the white walls of the house.

Teresa went on a pilgrimage to the area in 2007, with a friend called Ewa Cherner. Ewa has since been very helpful in sending me a copy of Teresa's book about the Kossak and Czerkawski families, and in describing their trip to Ukraine, including a brief visit to Meryszczów. She tells me that although they were there in July, 'the weather was rainy and cool.' Disappointingly, they saw nobody who might have been able to answer their many questions. She writes, 'The environment seemed to us quite monotonous and swampy, due to the large number of small rivers.' I think that Teresa, who was eight years younger than my father, had never been to Meryszczow before. 'Relying on stories told by her parents, Teresa pointed out a place not far from the road, on a small hill. Yet there were only the ruins of a quite depressing collective farm.'

Ewa included a handful of pictures of a rainy, featureless landscape that in Scotland we would call *dreich*, and the sad remnants of a few fairly modern structures, miscellaneous, barely recognisable bits of decaying metal and brick. If this is where the old house once stood, there seems little evidence of it now, but almost a hundred years have gone by since my father was born, war has passed over this land as it is passing over it again, and nature can reclaim buildings from the depredations of man with surprising speed, especially when those buildings have been associated with people and political ideologies that have fallen out of favour. It was a while before I noticed the single truly distinctive thing about one of these photographs, something that my father would have recognised instantly from his childhood: the characteristic stork platform, with two birds just visible, creatures still believed to bring good fortune to those who help them.

There is a more recent picture online from Meryszczów, of a building labelled the Kędzierski house. This is perched beside the main road through the village. It looks rather small and insignificant and it has no roofed turret. Many years ago, a contact called Valeriy Podolinnyy, who worked in the Lviv historical museum, very kindly send me some black and white photographs of this building, which he identified with my family home. He said it housed a nursery school at that time. Perhaps because of its position in the village, it has changed very little in the intervening period. The roof is made of tin, and this house too seems to sit on a slope so that it is larger from the back than from the front, but Teresa did not believe that this was the house her mother had loved so much. Ewa points out that it looks as though it was once the home of a wealthy farmer or estate manager. It certainly doesn't correspond with the manor house described in such detail, both by my father and Wanda Kossak, even allowing for changes of use, not least in where it is situated and what surrounds it.

An old but topographically accurate map, the Galizien und Lodomerien First Military Survey, drawn between 1779 and 1783, has a road running south through the settlement of Meryszczów, recognisable even today, with the Orthodox church and various other cottages alongside, but on this old map, there is a cluster of important buildings set well back from the road, to the west of the village, with a narrow driveway leading up to them. This seems a much more likely candidate for the Czerkawski house (and also for the site of the derelict collective farm whose remains Teresa and Ewa photographed in 2007). From a couple of surviving watercolours of the entrance to the Meryszczów estate from the 1920s, it's obvious that there was once an imposing entrance, with large gateposts, a driveway and a distant white walled, brown roofed building, such as my father and his aunt described.

For some of its history, Meryszczów seems to have been in the ownership of the Kędzierski family, but looking further back, one of the recorded owners is Marcin Czerkawski, son of Jacob and Katarzyna. His birth year is given as 1709, which places the Czerkawski ownership back in the seventeenth century. Benedict Czerkawski, born in 1763, spanned two centuries, and died in 1852, at the grand age of eighty-nine, having fathered a great many children, including Jozef Czerkawski, born in 1802, still listed as owning the estate in 1867. Many years ago a distant relative told me an apocryphal story about a legendary forebear who fathered many children, lived to a great age and died in a hunting accident. I've since wondered if Benedict was that man. In the 1700s, the Kędzierski family were living in nearby Przemyślany, but by the nineteenth century, there must have been some close relationship between them and the Czerkawskis, in all likelihood by marriage. It's feasible that at some point in its past, part of the estate had been given as a dowry, upon the marriage of one of the Czerkawski daughters to a Kędzierski son. In the 1890s, my great grandfather Władysław Czerkawski is already living there but Stanisław Kędzierski is still listed as a 'tabular owner'. He seems to have been the last of that family to claim ownership, before the estate reverted wholly to the Czerkawskis.

Teresa's mother described the house and the family's way of life there in some detail. Her father's bedroom and study was on the highest level, a bolt hole for Władysław. His study had a fireplace and, very unusually for the time and a great rarity when first installed, a coke furnace, one that was lit day and night in wintertime. On the main floor of the house, at the side facing away from the road, there was a dining room, with a drawing room leading out of it, and next to that, Anna's small boudoir, all of these rooms joined by double doors, much like British country houses of the time. In those days of hunting, shooting and heavy drinking, ladies treasured their boudoirs no less in Poland than in Scotland. There was a small library and also, perhaps in the other wing, two children's rooms: one for the girls and one for the boys.

On the ground floor, below the suites inhabited by the family, the cook and the butler had their rooms, with a separate domain for the housekeeper or chatelaine. Two other rooms were occupied by the bailiff or estate manager's family. The maids slept in the kitchen, which was situated next to a pantry. I get the impression of a house simply bursting with people. Down in this functional part of the house was a big hallway with a mangle and a cauldron for boiling potatoes for the pigs. Anna's eldest daughter, Wanda, could visualise the house exactly as it had been when she was a girl. From this hallway, stairs led to the veranda, with access to a butler's pantry, where they washed dishes and where the silver samovar simmered all day long. This was essential, because Władysław used to drink thirty cups of tea a day, a curious fact that was related not just by Wanda, but by my father too. The tea drinking habit persists in our family, since Władysław's grandson had the good fortune to marry an Irish girl.

Not, however, that the tea is ever drunk from a silver samovar.

To this house came Anna Brudzewska von Brause. The family always gave a nod towards her high status. 'Your great granny was a countess,' an elderly relative said to me once, much to my astonishment, verging on embarrassment. Me with my Yorkshire accent and my left wing sympathies too.

Well, perhaps not a countess, but little Anna would have been well aware that she came from a very distinguished family. Nevertheless, her father approved of the Czerkawskis, and she was happy at Meryszczów, presiding over her own establishment, as well as the samovar. According to her daughter, she was a great reader, she loved music, and she played the piano quite well. Education was prized among most Poles for sons and daughters alike. Children, even rural children, went to school and for a time, Anna had been at a boarding school in Kraków. She was, wrote Teresa, 'familiar with the local intellectuals' who must have participated in the literary and artistic gatherings of the time, some of them, like Wyspiański, rather less suitable than others.

It was here that Anna gave birth to her first daughter, Antonina Wanda, in 1896. She was always called Wanda, but the Antonina was appended because Wanda was a pagan name, of which the priest disapproved. It's certainly a very old Polish name and not at all of Christian origin, so perhaps he was right. Wanda Siemaszko was a well known actress of the day who had played a key role in one of Wyspiański's plays, and had been painted by him, wearing her costume from the play, so perhaps the name had a certain fashionable ring to it, especially for Anna.

Wanda remembered her father as a quiet man, firm with his children when need be, but always fair. He treated everyone with courtesy, whether they were his friends, his servants, the workers on the estate or, indeed, his children, who were taught the virtue of politeness above all things. He was a good landlord, keeping up to date with farming innovation, frequently travelling to Lwów and, significantly perhaps in view of his previous history, to Vienna. He subscribed to farming magazines and he imported modern equipment.

His eldest daughter also described him as being exceptionally gentle and loving with his wife. Although money was tight, as it invariably was for the minor *szlachta*, he never spared expense on books and sheet music for her. No portrait of Władysław has survived and there is one only of a youthful Anna, with her direct gaze, her slightly sulky mouth and her matronly satin gown. Wanda's later judgment on her mother as a 'frivolous coquette' may have been coloured by subsequent events in Anna's life, but it seems obvious that Władysław loved his wife very much and did his best to replicate the small luxuries she must have known, growing up at Korabniki. Among these considerations, he paid village woman handsomely to gather ant nests. They would bring them in baskets from the surrounding forests, to deposit them on the parkland surrounding the house. Anna had grown up listening to nightingales at Korabniki, she loved to hear them singing and they appreciated ant eggs.

Wanda was a favourite with her father as eldest daughters often are. Although the history of the Czerkawskis contains those of Orthodox and Roman Catholic persuasion, my family's branch were Roman Catholic, and the closest church would have been in Przemyślany where this first, much loved daughter was baptised. There was an historic Orthodox church dedicated to St Paraskeva in Meryszczów, a fine building which can still be seen to this day, and there's no doubt that Władysław would have been involved with ceremonies at this church from time to time, as my own grandfather was later involved with various ceremonies at the Orthodox church in Dziedziłow. The various branches of Christianity were, in this part of the world at least, fairly amicably interlinked.

Christenings often took place during the year following the birth of a child, since infancy could still be a precarious time. Wanda was a healthy and cheerful baby who looked very like her mother but was considerably more robust. Other children soon followed, four boys and another girl, but it was Wanda who was the favourite. He sometimes took her on his travels with him, and she remembered all her life that they had been to see a flea circus in Vienna, at the busy Volksprater, with its many stalls, taverns and coffee houses, already dominated by the Riesenrad of Third Man fame, where a sign proclaimed 'Stop! Stop! Flea Circus. The most curious exhibition in the world.' Flea circuses were bizarre but popular carnival attractions until the 1930s, and there's a Pathe News film in existence of a flea circus in Paris in 1949, with disturbingly large fleas hauling tiny carriages about and occasionally leaping towards the spectators. Wanda never forgot the weird magic of it.

Władysław was concerned for the education of all his children, sending his daughters, as they outgrew home and governess schooling, to a comfortable boarding school in Lwów, where Wanda took violin lessons and art classes with a Polish realist and romanticist painter called Stanisław Kaczor-Batowski who ran his own painting school in the city and whose work includes several vivid depictions of the Polish Winged Hussars. One fascinating aspect of this project for me, has involved a renewed understanding of many of my father's attitudes and endearing traits, that must have been deeply ingrained in him from birth. When we moved to Scotland in the 1960s and the headmaster at my new school had the temerity to ask Dad if he really wanted me to go to university 'because she'll only get married', my kind, gentle father immediately swung into outraged and autocratic *szlachta* mode, almost speechless with indignation that such an attitude (actually quite commonplace in Britain at the time) should exist.

'Why on earth not?' he asked, in disgust.

There were six children of this marriage, born over an exhausting eight years for Anna. There was a first son called Zbigniew, born around 1898. Next came Michał who died in infancy. He was followed by Bogusław, circa 1901. Another girl came along late in 1902 or very early in 1903, officially registered as Ludwika, but always called Ludmiła, or more frequently by her pet names of Ludka or Ludenka. She was, for the time being, the youngest sister. In January 1904, my grandfather Władysław was born in the sleigh. It was a remarkable beginning, and he would prove to be a remarkable man. All the children were sallow skinned and dark haired, with typically Slavic high cheekbones. They were a good looking family and the boys in particular were fearless to the point of recklessness.

If Anna and Władysław senior were not overly indulgent parents, nor were they particularly strict. The house was hardly big enough for that. The girls had to do all their own sewing and mending. They were, according to Wanda, whose memories were often coloured by a certain nostalgia, taught to be polite, generous, and brave, but she also remembered that she was instructed in how to 'be a lady', and was made to lie on boards for hours at a time, to straighten her back. Nevertheless, good humour and laughter must have been part of this crowded country childhood, with the strict upstairs downstairs demarcations of life in other European country houses impossible to observe with any precision. When my parents finally visited Poland and spent time with Wanda and her husband, Wanda whispered to my father that she was very surprised by how much my mother laughed.

'We laughed a lot at home,' she said to Julian. 'But the upper class English ladies I met over the years, at receptions and cultural events, only ever seemed to manage a faint (and no doubt faintly disapproving) smile.'

Władysław bought toys for his children, some of them educational, although any man who takes his daughter to see a flea circus and tries to entice nightingales into his garden for his wife's pleasure can't have been too serious-minded. Their food was simple but appetising enough, and Wanda remembered that the household all ate more or less the same meals. Władysław had 'rosół' (chicken broth with noodles) which was supposed to be healthy, every day, as well as the large quantities of tea provided by the samovar. He smoked constantly, as did so many people at the time, and managed the estate with the help of a steward who lived on the premises.

The girls were taught by their mother and later by a governess, before spending a few years at school in Lwów. There were plenty of books in the house and later they were free to read whatever they chose. Besides this, Anna taught her girls to sew and embroider, but mostly she taught them how to darn, a skill Wanda said was a lot more useful to her in later life than violin lessons. A pity, but perhaps such an active, outdoor girl was none too keen on scraping a tune from a violin or on darning for that matter. I get the impression that Wanda's early childhood was a happy one, with a freedom that few children of that time experienced. She may have been quieter and more religious than her siblings, but even more than reading and music, the love of Wanda's young life was horse riding. This was, after all, a cavalry family, with a long tradition of horsemanship that stretched back over hundreds of years, and the women were no exception. In her free time, of which there seems to have been plenty, Wanda rode, not side saddle, like a lady, but with her legs thrown over, clad in riding breeches, like a man. When her admiring artist husband-to-be sketched her later, he called her an Amazon. She climbed trees and in winter she skated and sleighed with her brothers. Ludmiła, by contrast, preferred to spend time in her mother's boudoir, engaging in less strenuous pursuits. Just as Wanda was her father's favourite, pretty Ludmiła was cherished by Anna, who was of a romantic disposition, and was not quite sure what to make of her other tomboy of a daughter.

Wanda was closest to Władysław, her youngest brother, and the feeling was mutual. She admitted that she and her sister Ludmiła became friends only as adults. Ludmiła was more conventionally pretty than Wanda, the typical 'bright young thing' who smoked, drank alcohol, and drove around in cars with headstrong young men. When I stayed with Wanda and her husband, Karol, in the 1970s, she showed me a heap of old photographs from her youth, among them her two handsome elder brothers and a picture of beautiful Ludka, perched on a wall. She's dressed in silk lounging pyjamas, she's holding a cigarette in a long, elegant holder and smiling enticingly at whoever is holding the camera. Her future husband, perhaps? Her friends must have envied her good fortune. For a while, at least.

As Wanda grew into a woman, her daughter Teresa observes that, 'She did not meet the beauty standards of her time. Her nose was too big, her lips were too wide, but she also had beautiful, brown eyes, thick dark hair and a charming smile.' The older she grew, the more talented as an equestrian she became. She always held herself well on a horse, all those years of lying on boards having the desired effect. It was this love of horse-riding that would attract her future husband, Karol Kossak, ironically, or so it must have seemed to Anna, who had been fond of Wspiański, another artist with a racy reputation. Before that marriage, however, the family would be disrupted in several unexpected ways. To understand how that came about, we have to find out a little more about the man my father always called 'Uncle Julian'.

CHAPTER EIGHT

An Unexpected Inheritance

Now, I need to stitch another rich and strange thread into this tapestry. I've tried and failed to find a portrait of this particular Julian Czerkawski. He was a collector of old Polish art and antiquities, a medical doctor and a politician who represented Poland in the Austro-Hungarian parliament in Vienna. I feel a portrait must exist somewhere, but I haven't found one. One of the first documents I came across in my search for the Czerkawski family history was a long newspaper article about him. When he died, obituaries were published in Polish and Austrian newspapers since he was well regarded in both countries.

This Julian Czerkawski, who gave his Christian name to my father, was born to Michał Czerkawski and his wife Antonina Dobrowolska, on January 12th, 1831, in a place called Olesko, some 60 kilometres North-east of Lwów. Julian's impressive tombstone, in the overgrown cemetery in Dziedziłow, gives his birth year as 1834. It's hard to judge which year is accurate, but since the hand written public records, the entries written at the time of his birth and his contemporary obituaries all state 1831, the earlier date is probably the correct one. The surname Dobrowolska, meaning 'good will', was common among converts from Judaism, of which there were significant numbers at this time. Noble men and women married wealthy converts and then kept their origins secret, although it was an open secret, since everyone knew what the name meant. It reminds me a little of the way the impoverished English nobility would later marry American heiresses and absorb them, or try to, into the peculiarly privileged and occasionally eccentric world they took for granted. When I recently had my DNA tested, the results (more precise than I expected) indicated plenty of Celtic and Scandinavian from the Irish/Yorkshire side of the family, but just as much Ashkenazi Jewish as the anticipated Central and Eastern European DNA, confirming something I had long suspected.

When I first saw the name Olesko, I assumed that it was a town, and that the couple were away from home for some reason. A little research reveals that Olesko is a picturesque rural area, 75 kilometres slightly to the North-east of what is now Lviv. Even now, the village is a scattered settlement of cottages and small farms, with a current population of about 1500, surrounding an equally picturesque mediaeval castle, one of the oldest in Galicia. Like something out of a fairy-tale, it is perched on a fine defensive height, with an eighteenth-century Capuchin Monastery sitting just below it.

Why Michał and his wife were living there when Julian was born, or indeed where, precisely, I didn't know for quite some time. I wondered if Antonina had connections at Olesko. Perhaps they weren't so much living there as visiting her relatives. Julian's birth month was January and travelling through the snows was impractical for a heavily pregnant woman, as my poor great grandmother would later discover. But then my friend and indefatigable family history researcher Ewa Czerkawska came across mention of Michał as a 'possessor' of Olesko, which changed my perspective.

I found an antique print of the castle on eBay. It looks like something out of a fairy-tale. It had been the birthplace of Jan Sobieski III, the King of Poland from 1674 to 1696. At this time, Poland elected its kings. I'm surprised that the concept of an elective monarchy seems so bizarre to some of my British friends, but such a system was not uncommon, even among our near neighbours in Ireland. Jan was allegedly born at Olesko between 2 and 3 o'clock on 17th August, 1629, at yet another time of great turmoil, involving fierce skirmishes between the invading Turks of the Ottoman Empire and the Poles who were, as ever, attempting to hold them back, assisted from time to time by the Ruthenians and the semi-independent Cossacks. In fact during the seventeenth century a Polish-Lithuanian-Ruthenian Commonwealth was proposed, but never came to fruition. There was little peace to be had, and what there was had to be snatched from the jaws of war. My grandfather would have known all about this, as would his father before him, as do those who live there now. I remember whenever people asked my father about the lost members of his family and what had happened to them, he tended to reply, drily, 'lead poisoning'. It wasn't entirely true, but life was precarious at best.

Even as early as 1831, when Julian was born here, the castle at Olesko had seen better days and no single family was in complete possession. Rather, inheritance and successive dowries, coupled with a certain amount of squabbling about rights, probably meant that several families, including Julian's father, could and did lay claim to this crumbling structure. In 1838, an earthquake caused further significant damage to the castle, which nevertheless would go on to survive this upheaval, two world wars and a lightning strike. It is now a museum of Polish and Ukrainian arts and artefacts and also has an extensive collection of wood sculptures. For now.

All of which makes me wonder if Julian's parents, who must have told him about his birthplace, and who may even have taken him back there, inspired his later love of Polish art and traditions. It was true that little of the original grandeur of its interiors would have survived, and most of the precious artefacts had been removed long ago, but a few of them may have remained. In fact I sometimes wonder if a small portion of Julian's later remarkable collection of old Polish art and antiquities may have come from Olesko, courtesy of King Jan Sobieski and his wife, found in situ and squirrelled away by Julian's appreciative parents. But since the collection in question no longer exists, except in handed-down memories, we have no way of knowing.

In subsequent years, this branch of the Czerkawski family had their main residence in Lwów, even though there were still strong connections with the family home at Meryszczów. A bright young man, Julian studied philosophy at Lwów University, attended Kraków University and then left Poland to study Medicine and Surgery in Vienna. In 1864, he was awarded the title of Doctor of Medical Sciences in that city. He served as a medical colonel in the

Austrian army for a couple of years but from 1866 onwards, he specialised as an oculist and ran his own medical practice back in his beloved Lwów.

He was interested in politics and gradually began to move in that direction, in tandem with his medical career. He was, by our standards, very conservative, although 'traditional' might be a better description, but he also became a Land Health Councillor at a time when many conscientious estate owners were trying to improve their land and, by extension, the bitter poverty of those working on it. He belonged to a group of Galician landowners called the Podolians who agitated for Galician autonomy in the face of almost constant unrest. Even more controversially, they sought to limit the rights of the Jewish and Ruthenian populations. They wanted to limit the laws involving the official use of the Ukrainian language, in favour of Latin, which was ostensibly a nod to the old Sarmatian tradition, and to fairness, but not much of one, given that few Ruthenians or Poles for that matter, knew that language or wanted to speak it. The Podolians opposed electoral reform and, above all, they wanted to maintain the existing structure of land ownership in Galicia. His politics were undeniably patriarchal. To facilitate at least some of this, Julian set his sights on the parliament in Vienna.

From 1871 to 1879 he was a councillor in the city of Lwów and during that period he represented his city as member of the Austrian State Council, becoming a deputy in the Austrian parliament from 1879 to April 1885, the closest adviser to the president of the Polish Circle there. He would have seen himself chiefly as a patriotic Pole, promoting autonomy for Galicia at the expense of the Ukrainian and Jewish populations, with a desire to see the restoration of the old Polish Commonwealth. These somewhat dubious views run parallel with various accounts of him as a caring and generous landowner and an enthusiastic agricultural reformer. In short, he was a Polish nobleman of his time.

One of his obituaries states that after 1870, he 'bought the estate at Dziedziłow', although since another account speaks of his 'native Dziedzilow' the estate may already have belonged to relatives. Another correspondent who had known my grandfather well is careful to point out that it was an 'inherited tenancy'. Whatever the connection, Julian became owner of the heritable tenancy of the estate of Dziedziłów, where he eventually settled permanently in 1890. From that date, he withdrew from public life and political activity and focused solely on the estate and the large manor house that stood there, containing his growing collection of Polish books, art and artefacts, of which King Jan Sobieski and his wife would have approved. They may even have recognised a few of the items as their own.

In 1881, the village of Dziedziłow, thirty kilometres East of Lwów, was a place of fine fertile soil with a lake used for breeding carp, a Polish tradition since the thirteenth century. Poles are very fond of eating this bony but tasty fish, especially at Christmas. In this year, there were 159 Roman Catholics, 889 Greek Orthodox Ruthenians – i.e. the vast majority were Ukrainians – and 161 Jewish people living and working on and around the estate. There was an

Orthodox church and a primary school with one teacher, a school which my father would later attend for a while, before events, domestic and political, changed his life for ever.

The village was said to have been founded in 1441, but it is difficult to discover the ancient history of this place. The same military map from 1779, where I found Meryszczów, shows the village of Dziedziłow on the shore of a large lake, with a prominent island. Tradition tells of an island upon which stood a castle belonging to notorious troublemaker and adventurer, Stanisław Stadnicki, nicknamed the Devil of Łancut. Born in 1551, this rogue led a riotous and violent life, and died at the age of fifty-nine, in retreat after one battle too many, taking some five hundred soldiers to their deaths with him. In typical bad boy fashion, he has featured in various Polish films and novels as well as, in grim old age, in a painting by nineteenth-century Polish artist Jan Matejko. According to my father's account, when part of that large lake at Dziedziłow was drained and converted into excellent pasture, the remains of the Devil's castle could be seen. Perhaps some of those stones found their way into one or two of the older houses on the estate. Perhaps they brought a certain amount of ill luck with them.

The 1881 account says that the estate is 'now in the hands of Starzeński's heirs'. By that time, it seems to have been in the hands of Julian Czerkawski, because his later obituary describes him 'retiring to his own village' around that time. Other documents refer to him as the 'owner of the inherited property of Dziedziłow'. He had never married and was without children, so perhaps he himself had become one of Starzeński's heirs, or was at least a 'heritable tenant' – i.e. a tenancy that could be passed on after death – via the complexities of previous dowries and inheritances. Certainly Dziedziłow was in his gift, to leave to whomever he chose. His choice was a surprising one and had unforeseen consequences for the family.

During Uncle Julian's time, there was a forty-roomed mansion house in the old Polish style with, according to family tradition and little else, those characteristically yellow walls, painted in the colour called *kaiserschmarrn*. This was the pancake known as the Emperor's Mess, after Emperor Franz Jósef's favourite and most delicious pudding. When I was a child, my father used to sing me a sad little lullaby about a princess who lived in a house made of butter, a big yellow house full of wonderful things. Later, I wondered if his own father had sung it, remembering the old manor house at Dziedziłow. My father had seen sketches of it but there are no photographs. He said that, from the entrance, it looked like a long, low building with a small central tower, but in fact the main entrance was on the first floor because, just like the smaller house at Meryszczów, this manor house too had been built into the hillside. From the other side, where the ground sloped away, it was more imposing. It had stone foundations and was built of brick, plastered and painted. The main building had a more ornate central section, rising higher than the rest, and there were wings on either side with cellars underneath. But my father had never really known the house. Had never possessed it to lose it. Like Maxim de Winter's Mandalay, it was no more, lost to fire. Only lullabies and the cellars remained of that splendid mansion, an intriguing footprint for a child to play in. And an ice house that was still in use.

It was in this house, at Dziedziłow, in the later years of the nineteenth century, that Great Uncle Julian began to follow his lifelong passion for collecting Polish pictures, weapons, porcelain and many other precious things, including gold uniform braid, frogging and especially those ancient heavily embroidered *kontusz* sashes that were Turkish in origin, as was so much Polish weaponry. He had a passion for those, and as a textile collector myself, I wish they had survived. There was a library in the house, stuffed with precious volumes. In a regretful account from 1926, when it was no more, and when a deputation had already been sent from Soviet Russia, to see what might be preserved, (very little, not surprisingly) we learn that there had been a large collection of historical books, as well as a picture gallery. The house had woodcuts and weaponry, historical and even archaeological collections. Most of it was amassed by Julian in Lwów, Kraków, Vienna and elsewhere. There was, reputedly, a suit of the old Winged Hussar armour, bristling with eagle feathers, the sound of which had so terrorised the Ottoman enemy at the gates of Vienna. It would have been characteristic of the man to acquire such a treasure, one with so many associations with old Poland.

Latterly, Julian lived there alone, with a limited staff, and with short visits to Lwów, to bookshops and antiquarian dealers. In the privacy of his home, he might dress in the old Sarmatian costume, which would certainly have been recognisable to King Jan Sobieski, but he also favoured so-called 'peasant dress' with embroidered linen shirts, the obligatory tall leather boots, and, of course, the fine moustache. I often think of him as a performer, an eccentric who liked to live his literature and his history, but he was also something of an idealist and a romantic – a contradiction of a man. He was reputed to be a first class, hard-headed manager and, like his nephew at Meryszczów, he expanded the estate and improved it, until it consisted of some 2000 productive acres.

He believed in the virtues of the Polish Commonwealth and wished for nothing so much as to resurrect it. In the manner of those old *szlachta* lords and ladies, he was tremendously hospitable and welcomed visitors young and old, so he was certainly no recluse. He even treated patients at home although 'not everybody' remarked my father when he wrote an account of this relative he had never known. He would treat a poverty stricken smallholder without payment, while autocratically rejecting anyone whose standards of politeness and respect didn't match his own, however much money they might offer. When I think about my own father, tolerant and kindly as he was, the unforgiveable sin in his eyes was a lack of generosity, both of spirit and materially. He simply couldn't abide meanness.

In 1900 we find another letter from Julian, respectfully addressed to a priest. I have an archive image of it, the handwriting clear, neat and elegant, devastatingly personal as all past handwriting is, when unexpectedly recovered. Even now, gazing at a scan of it, I can feel the hairs on the back of my neck prickling a little. It is addressed to a canon priest, calling him the equivalent of 'The Right Reverend Esquire'. We would probably have called him 'Monsignor' back when I was attending a Catholic school. The friend who translated this for me says that it is in 'lovely, old fashioned language, using very respectful and noble words.'

It's almost impossible to translate this into modern Polish, never mind English, but the letter deals with the death of a woman who was clearly known to Julian. He asks the priest to give a date and time for her funeral and to notify the grave digger to prepare a place for her. 'The deceased didn't have any money, so I will cover the funeral costs,' he says. Her name was Leopoldina Schneider and she was forty-six. Her husband had done occasional work as a farm manager for a family in 'Milatyn and Nahorce'. These were villages close to Dziedziłow so the family were well known to Julian. Leopoldina died a couple of hours after receiving the holy sacraments. 'I also enclose a note with confirmation of her baptism performed by Father Jaworowski in absentia of the canon priest.' This suggests that she was baptised on her deathbed as well as receiving the last sacraments, perhaps from the equivalent of a curate. The letter was written at Dziedziłow, and dated 6th January 1900. Julian signs himself 'Your obedient servant, Czerkawski', the usual confident single signature that my grandfather would use in his turn. Why did he pay for the funeral of this destitute woman? She was considerably younger than he, so perhaps he had known her as a child. Perhaps he had treated her in her last illness.

Julian may have had no children himself, but he was a warm and welcoming uncle to the family. Especially to my grandfather. Anna and Władysław's children were growing and thriving, and frequent visits to Great Uncle Julian were one of the more entertaining features of their childhood. Fifty kilometres was quite a long way for children to travel, although perhaps their parents accompanied them. They would have gone by carriage in summer, although perhaps the older boys rode, or travelled on sleighs in the snowy winters. The three brothers, tall Zbigniew, stocky Bogusław and Władysław, the youngest and most wayward, travelled there more frequently than the girls, and Uncle Julian tolerated all kinds of mischief not to say savagery. According to Władysław's later accounts, one of the games was called 'killing pigs' and involved Bogusław slicing into his little brother's neck with a penknife, whereupon Władysław squealed like a very convincing pig.

The most memorable event from that time at Dziedziłow happened when Julian was receiving important visitors from Lwów. They had arrived in a fancy carriage, pulled by four trotting horses. Carriage and horses had been temporarily 'parked' under a shelter near the house, before being taken to the stables. My grandfather, who must have been no more than five years old at the time, had managed to purloin a starting pistol from somewhere, clambered up onto the roof of the shelter, and fired it.

'To see what would happen,' he said later, by way of explanation, although I think he might have been egged on by his brothers.

What happened was that they recovered bits of the carriage and four unhurt but frightened horses, some miles away from the house. Far from being angry, Uncle Julian found the whole episode amusing. My grandfather was a favourite, and would remain so for what was left of Julian's life.

1910 was the start of a difficult time for the family. Anna's husband died during that year, leaving her a young widow with five children ranging in ages from teens down to six year old Władysław. That same year, Julian surprised an intruder in his house. The attacker stabbed him and then escaped into the night, although he was subsequently caught and tried. Julian sustained serious injuries, but clung to life for a while, until he too died in 1911 and was buried at Dziedziłow.

In 1989 the National Library of Austria sent me a copy of a long and fulsome obituary. 'Julian Czerkawski burned with love for his country, although he was also modest and he did not seek the limelight. He was Doctor of three faculties, he was uncommonly erudite and was always interested in public matters. He was sent as delegate to the state council in Vienna. During that time Czerkawski made a speech in defence of our Polish rights, and finished with a raised, clenched fist. The Austrians were offended and complained bitterly about his bad manners! Having offered what he could, he retired to his own village, where he began to interest himself in the forlorn peasantry, his poverty and ignorance. Here he began to follow his earlier passion for collecting Polish art and artefacts which began to fill this old bachelor's stately home. He had once loved Lwów but this affection waned as time passed. His comrades in arms grew grey, his old, respected opponents went away, and he did not want to associate with the new people, finding their behaviour pretentious. He felt better in Dziedziłow where he had made an old Polish Commonwealth of his own, one that was evident in every corner of his many rooms.'

I think Julian hankered after something that was gone, never to return, an idealist to the end. Perhaps he saw something of that same love of history in one of Anna's children. After his death, much to the surprise and possibly even resentment of the rest of the family, it was revealed that Julian had left the tenancy of the large estate of Dziedziłow to his youngest great nephew, my grandfather, the culprit with the starting pistol, and still only seven years old.

CHAPTER NINE

A Very Competent Manager

Great grandmother Anna, in her late thirties, was a widow with five children to bring up, of whom the eldest, Wanda, was still only fourteen years old. Self-sufficiency was not something she would ever have needed to contemplate. She was never going to be the feisty woman of contemporary fiction. Before Anna's year of mourning was up, Uncle Julian had died too, and her youngest son, just seven years old, a bright and charming child, but full of mischief, had inherited the estate at Dziedziłow, fifty kilometres away. That meant five children, two estates and a great many people reliant on those estates for their everyday survival. Anna was overwhelmed by the responsibilities involved. She was a wealthy woman by most standards, but much of that wealth was tied up in land. There would have been little disposable income, unless the estates were well run. What on earth was she to do? How could she manage?

When an offer of marriage came along from a competent and not unattractive man, I can well understand why she might have said yes, although her time of mourning for her husband would hardly have been over. The fact that the man also happened to be a much younger farm manager on one of the family estates came as something of a shock to her friends and relatives.

Jan Honig was a Czech by birth, an interesting and intelligent young man. His passion was dairying, cheese-making in particular. He was born in Moravia in the East of Czechia, bordering on Poland. Later, he graduated from a dairy school in Thurgau, in Switzerland, where he had gone to learn how to make a form of Tilsit cheese. I know very little about his family background, but it's safe to assume that it was agricultural and that he had an interest in dairy farming from a young age. Until the 1800s, cereal cultivation had predominated in Thurgau, just as it had in much of Poland. When the new railways allowed for the importation of cheap Ukrainian grain, which in turn threatened their livelihoods, many smallholders in Switzerland turned to dairy production, but didn't know how to conserve the milk, beyond making butter and traditional fermented products. Cheese was the obvious solution. The Swiss began with Emmenthal, and then, in 1893, began to explore the possibilities of a delicious form of cheese that had originated in Tilsit in East Prussia. It was softer than Emmenthal but – as I can testify, having found some in Lidl as part of the research for this book – exceptionally tasty.

Jan Honig graduated from the Rutti Zollikofen dairy school in Switzerland and then he began work as a teacher at the First National Dairy School in Rzeszów in Poland. He had been one of its co-founders, together with Jan Licznerski, Tadeusz Rylski, after whom the school is still named and Franciszek Górecki, who would later be one of the witnesses at Jan and Anna's wedding in Lwów. Jan even ran the school himself for a short time. I thought at first that he might have worked at Meryszczów, but now I think it's much more likely that he was already at Dziedziłow when my grandfather inherited the estate. Julian Czerkawski had been in favour of agricultural improvements, right from his days as Land Health Councillor, through to his retirement to Dziedziłow. He clearly saw prospects for land reform and the introduction of dairying and it made sense for him to employ a talented young man. Perhaps Jan Honig himself saw better prospects there, where he could focus on his beloved cheesemaking. He would have come with excellent references from his colleagues at the National School of Dairying. Researching this so many years later, I'm intrigued by the coincidence that my late father eventually specialised in dairy research.

Anna was struggling to cope with just about everything without her husband and it may even have been the case that, before his death, Julian had asked Jan to help her out. When Julian himself died and her youngest son inherited the estate at Dziedziłow, a devastated Anna would inevitably have been thrown together with, and perhaps physically attracted to, this capable young steward.

I remember my surprise at discovering just how young my grandfather had been when he inherited the estate where my father would later spend his childhood. It was one of those odd revelations you often find in the middle of family history research, where all your assumptions come tumbling down. It can be a date, or a letter, or a casual reference. We are storytellers of our own lives. We do it all the time, in real life or on social media, telling tales about everyday occurrences. But that means that when we come across random collections of facts that puzzle us, our natural tendency is to piece them together into a plausible story. I've done it more than once in telling this story, only to have my whole carefully constructed jigsaw puzzle fall apart, because of one little prod from reality. And so, you begin all over again, realising that the picture isn't quite what you thought it was.

In her account of her childhood, Wanda, somewhat grudgingly, calls Jan Honig the 'saviour of the estate' and to a large extent he was. Whether he was Anna's saviour or not is a moot point and one that only the couple themselves could have clarified. On 30th November, 1911, Jan Honig and Anna Czerkawska were married in the Church of St Nicholas in Lwów. Significantly, they didn't marry in the Catholic church at Przemyślany, which was much closer to Meryszczów, perhaps because there would have been a certain amount of disapproval. Jan was a professional man, with an excellent command of his vocation, but he was not one of the *szlachta* and the gossip would have been unkind, to say the least.

After her father's death, Wanda stated baldly that her happy childhood 'came to an abrupt end'. Around fourteen or fifteen years old, she stayed at school in Lwów for a while, going home to Meryszczów during the holidays, but it soon became obvious that her rather frail mother could not manage without her. What this 'frailty' amounted to is hard to say, because Anna would live on for another fourteen years, but Anna Danuta was born to Jan and Anna in 1912, so this last, late pregnancy may have triggered some of her ill health. Wanda was inclined to blame her brothers for not taking on the responsibility of managing the land themselves, but looking at their probable dates of birth, they would have been too young for such an undertaking. For inexperienced boys, looking after not one but two big estates, fifty kilometres apart, would have been impossibly challenging, and Jan was the obvious candidate for what was, after all, a skilled job.

In the case of the two eldest, they were still at school. My grandfather Władysław would have been at home, along with Ludmiła. The *szlachta* favoured boarding schools for their older boys and girls, but younger children were kept at home and taught either by their mothers, or by governesses, often foreigners, employed to give them a knowledge of other languages and customs. There are nineteenth-century accounts of Scottish governesses working in Poland, while French was still the favoured second language of many wealthy Poles, even though most of them could also speak German. In the 1970s, when I visited my surviving older relatives in Warsaw and elsewhere, we communicated in French, because my school French was better than my limited Polish, while many of them still spoke that language fluently. Given my grandfather's later love for England and its literature, I sometimes wonder if he may have had the benefit of an English governess for a time.

The Czerkawski sons were traditionally sent to school at Chyrów, a hundred kilometres west of Lwów. Run by the Jesuits, it was a college with a fine reputation. The Jesuits certainly valued scholarship. The academy's library was particularly good, including mediaeval manuscripts, collections of eighteenth-century maps, and many rare scholarly works. I'm not sure what this form of boarding school education was like for the boys. After all, these were future cavalrymen who would be trained in the arts of war. It does, however, sound as though Chyrów was more comfortable and a good deal less austere than its English equivalent at the time. The school could accommodate some four hundred students. It had a natural science department with a botanical garden attached, a theatre and good sports facilities. There was comfortable sleeping accommodation with modern plumbing and electricity, and with plenty of space for socialising. There was even a bakery attached to the flour mill. Like so much else in this part of the world, it no longer exists in its previous form. At the time of the Soviet Invasion of 1939, the Chyrów Library contained over 50,000 volumes and items of cultural heritage. In that year, the Academy was 'liquidated' by the Soviet authorities and its library, with all its collections, was entirely destroyed.

My father would probably have gone there too, had war and invasion not intervened. It wouldn't have been a certainty though. He told me that there were also plans for him to study to become an artist, and although he had followed in his family footsteps in his love of horses, perhaps his parents, his father in particular, were already thinking that a career as a cavalryman was not for him. They may have had plans to send him to Chyrów for a few years and then to Warsaw or Kraków to study painting. Throughout his life, he was a talented hobby artist, working mostly in watercolours, although he also had a knack for sketching cartoons, acquired from his Aunt Wanda's artist husband, Karol Kossak.

Where Jan and Anna's marriage was concerned, the Czerkawski children wondered, and carried on wondering, why Anna had agreed to the match. Jan was twenty-nine and she would have been thirty-nine. This gap in ages, while insignificant for an older man marrying a younger woman, even now causes a few raised eyebrows. It seemed scandalous at this time, in this place. Wanda describes the marriage as undertaken 'to save the estate' but this leaves so much unsaid. If Jan had been working for Julian at Dziedziłow, she would certainly have met him earlier, when the family visited his favourite uncle. But the deaths of her husband and Uncle Julian coupled with her young son's unexpected inheritance all meant that she became even more reliant on him. She had grown up in a milieu in which there was always some more powerful, more confident man to lean on. She may have thought her own upbringing at Korabniki strict, as perhaps it was in terms of freedom, but she would have been shielded from many of the harsh realities of life. Her first marriage was very happy. Would her new husband even imagine paying people for ant nests, so that his wife could listen to the nightingales singing? Would he, while drinking his forty cups of tea from a silver samovar, be sociable, indulge Anna in trips to the city, buy a piano and the music to play on it, provide books, clothes, jewellery for her? Would he, when requested, leave her to her feminine pursuits in her boudoir? Somehow, I doubt it. Jan was competent, capable and energetic, I think she was afraid of the future, and she undoubtedly needed him. Was she attracted to him, and he to her? It's very likely, but I also think that any of the youthful romance she had with her first husband had fled with him and the nightingales.

The year after their marriage, around the time of the birth of their daughter, Jan changed his name from Honig to the much more Polish sounding Hanakowski, so perhaps he too was uncomfortable with the perceived differences between them, uncomfortable with having acquired a ready made and somewhat hostile family. I gaze at my sole photograph of Anna and wish I could ask her about it. I have no image of Jan, although, thanks to her son, I now have several pictures of his daughter, Anna Danuta, striking images of her as a young woman, a round faced, dark-eyed brunette with a lovely smile. I know how I would write, or attempt to write, a fictional account of the complexities of this relationship, of what Jan and Anna might have had to cope with, but I don't know how accurate it would be. I do know that as an adult, their daughter Danuta sent a little picture of herself to Jan dedicating it to 'my beloved father' which tells us something of what his daughter felt for him.

The successive deaths of Władysław and Uncle Julian, followed by Anna's speedy marriage to Jan, seemed to trigger a deep sense of unrest in the household, an unrest that only mirrored what was going on in the world outside. Jan may have saved Meryszczów, but his relationship with the children was far from easy. My father remarked that his own father would always refer to Jan as 'stepfather', never as 'father'. When Danuta was born, the atmosphere in the house at Meryszczów became, as Wanda describes it, 'rather grim' and Anna's health seemed to be worsening by the day. She may have suffered from post natal depression.

In some later documents, the child's birth place is officially quoted as Dziedziłow, which may have been the case, since the couple would certainly have travelled between the two estates. There had been too much upheaval in Anna's life and this last, late baby, much loved as she was, had only created more worry. Her new husband was managing two estates at once and the responsibilities involved would have left little time for the kind of care that Anna had come to expect. Wanda, therefore, left her school in Lwów and returned to Meryszczów so that she could look after her mother. Perhaps it was this period, and the sense that her horizons were narrowing, that gave her a certain resentment towards the brothers who would have been away at school and well removed from what was going on at home.

According to Wanda's own account, it was not a happy time. She and her mother had never been as close as Anna and Ludmiła. She had been her father's favourite, not Anna's. Although she claimed to love her mother and her siblings, and was deeply attached to the house and everything around it, including the dogs and especially the horses, she found the atmosphere there oppressive and took every opportunity to escape, visiting friends and cousins whenever she was sure that her mother could spare her. Meryszczów was her 'favourite place in the whole world' she said, but she and her stepfather were not on good terms. Looking at it from Jan's point of view, the tensions between him and the Czerkawski children must have been something of a nightmare. He was not their father, he was a young man, and the older children in particular would have been lacking in tact or empathy where he was concerned. As well as mutinous step-children, and (presumably) various household servants who couldn't see why they should treat him as the master of the house, following Władysław's death, he also had to cope with a sickly wife, a newborn daughter and the running of two estates, with all that that entailed. He was in an unenviable position, and I sympathise with him more than the older members of my family ever did.

Besides, he was their saviour in more ways than one.

When the Great War started, there was deep unrest between Ukrainians and Poles. This was something that had flared up in the past, and would continue to do so. These were heavily disputed borderlands with the disputes sometimes escalating in the bloodiest way possible. Great grandfather Władysław had been on good terms with his Ruthenian neighbours, but the family were warned that, even though they were not under threat from their tenants and neighbours, they would be in extreme danger from those fighting men who might be passing through. This was no idle warning. In 1914, only fifty kilometres away, the Front passed through the village of Dziedziłow, and my grandfather's inheritance, the house and the collection that Julian had spent half a lifetime building was burned to the ground. Anyone who got in the way would have been destroyed as well. The only good thing was that Julian was not alive to see it happening.

Sensibly heeding the warnings of well disposed local people, Jan decided that the safest thing to do would be to move his new family, including the Czerkawski children, his wife, and little Danuta, to Czechia, where he still had friends and relatives, until the situation calmed down. The party probably consisted of Jan and Anna, Wanda, Ludmiła, Władysław, still only ten years old, and baby Danuta. The two older brothers would have stayed at school. It was a blessing, and very much to Jan's credit, that he found a place of safety for them. It was Wanda's second trip abroad, the first being to Vienna with her father, and she admitted that she enjoyed their stay very much. She liked the country, the people they met, the order and cleanliness and the 'nice views'. I don't know where they stayed, but it is very likely that they went to Moravia, where Jan was born. Luckily, the estate was spared the worst of the looting and eventually they decided that it was safe to go home to Meryszczów.

CHAPTER TEN

Battles, Marriages
and Deaths

There followed a few years of relative peace for the family, although, as so often for Poland and Ukraine, it would prove to be yet another calm before the inevitable storm. Wanda describes her brothers at this time as 'reckless and unpredictable.' Well, perhaps they were. But trying to piece together some kind of timeline for all this, I reached the conclusion that they were just young men trying to have a bit of fun, at a time when the future seemed uncertain and when the country was full of unrest. She accused them of playing Russian roulette, although in his later accounts, my father had no memory of anything so reckless, even though he was close to his uncles, and told tales of other examples of wild behaviour. Firing starting pistols over the top of carriage horses was not the only misdemeanour. More believably, Wanda also said that they indulged in gambling, going around with girls and taking no interest at all in managing the estate. I'm sure they did go around with girls, whenever they had the opportunity. They were good looking lads and the girls probably liked to go around with them. It would also be true to say that they had other things to occupy their minds, but there was a sense in which their whole lives were becoming a game of Russian roulette, and just as randomly deadly.

In 1918, the two younger brothers, Władysław and Bogusław, aged fourteen and seventeen, ran away from the Jesuits at Chyrów, to join their elder brother in defending the city of Lwów against the Ukrainian forces, in what became known as the Battle of Lemberg.

This battle is sometimes called the 'last civilised conflict' in Polish history, civilised mostly because both sides lacked heavy weapons, and there were fewer than four hundred civilian casualties. It was not an invasion, so much as a conflict between two populations of a disputed territory, and the relationship between them had been uneasily intertwined for hundreds of years. Perhaps this explains why both sides tried hard not to destroy the city they loved, and, in stark contrast to the current Russian invasion, the most important infrastructure buildings, such as hospitals, water and gas works, were deliberately avoided. Local ceasefire agreements were signed daily, and there were several bizarre incidents in which Polish and Ukrainian soldiers played football or drank vodka together during ceasefires. Against this background, the much celebrated WW1 Christmas Eve truce between German and British soldiers seems less extraordinary. Bolesław Czerny wrote that during one of these ceasefires the Ukrainian commander of one outpost spent so much time carousing with a group of Poles that he overslept and woke up only after the latest ceasefire had ended. Another ceasefire was hurriedly signed between the combatants to allow the Ukrainian officer to return safely to his unit. All of which sounds like a dangerous game beside which Russian Roulette pales into insignificance.

The violence and disruption, however, were very real. The siege of the city was broken in November 1918. After the Polish takeover of the city, there were a great many Jewish casualties, when some soldiers and groups of criminals ran riot, looting and burning and targeting Jewish businesses in particular. Not very civilised at all, and many innocent people died or were injured. A significant number of the rioters were arrested and punished when order was restored, but the battle for overall control of Lwów lasted for some six months and came to an end only in May 1919. All three Czerkawski brothers were wounded during this conflict, but the eldest, Zbigniew, was badly injured. He lost a lung, which would make him prone to serious illness for the rest of his life.

In 1920, the Poles fought Russian invaders at the battle of Zadwórze, a Pyrrhic victory if ever there was one. They stopped the Russian advance, but the Polish forces were almost annihilated. I doubt very much if the brothers were involved in this battle, not least because they survived and most of the Polish combatants didn't. Zbigniew, in his early twenties, would be at home trying to recover his health, Bogusław, aged nineteen or so, would have been expected to assist his badly injured elder brother in helping to care for the estate at Meryszczów, and Władysław, still only sixteen, would have been ordered back to school for a year or two by his mother and stepfather, in an effort to keep him reasonably safe until he could come into his inheritance.

Most of the work would have devolved on the resourceful Jan Hanakowski, without whom, it is safe to say, they would have been in real trouble. Meanwhile, this continual unrest was having adverse effects on both estates and the considerable numbers of people who were reliant on them for their lives and livelihoods. As ever, there was little disposable income and successful agriculture does not go well with constant upheaval and the depredations of war. I think poor Jan must have had his work cut out for him.

Once my grandfather was old enough to plan for his future at Dziedzilow, he wondered where he should live. Nothing now remained of the yellow house and its collection, except the cellars, and the ice house down by the lake, but there were plenty of other buildings, not least the old estate manager's house, dating from well before Julian's manor house, a building that Uncle Julian had used to store produce from the estate. My grandfather decided that this would be his home, and set about planning and supervising renovation work. The Hanakowskis already had a house at a nearby village called Feliksa although I think Anna preferred to spend time at Meryszczów, which she still saw as her real home. Besides, her two elder daughters were living there. What Zbigniew felt about this is not recorded, but it may have been another source of dissent between the Czerkawskis and their stepfather.

The oldest part of the manager's house at Dziedzilow was solid stone, with an enormous chimney, which suggests that this had been the original manor, the residence of one of those earlier noblemen who owned the estate before the bigger mansion was built. In describing this much loved house where he had spent the first ten years or so of his life, my father hazarded that parts of it may have been some three hundred years old. As soon as he could, my grandfather threw himself and all his enthusiasm into the project of transforming it into a comfortable family home. These plans included an extension of brick and plaster, painted white, and some modern conveniences although the constraints of rural living meant that nothing was quite as comfortable as city life.

For a while, Jan travelled between the two estates, doing what he could to maintain both, but it must have been increasingly clear to him that the young heirs were determined to take over, Zbigniew almost immediately and Władysław as soon as he was of age. It was frustratingly clear to him too that the boys were far from experienced in farming and that Zbigniew was not nearly as fit as he might have been. Jan's position as Anna's husband gave him a certain status, but when push came to shove, her sons would take precedence. Meanwhile, a resentful Bogusław was given the consolation prize of a small estate of two hundred acres, a few kilometres from Dziedziłow, which he took possession of in 1923, when he reached his majority.

In 1924, my twenty-year-old grandfather met my grandmother, Łucja Szapera, at a ball in Lwów. She was sweet faced, with thick, dark, naturally wavy hair and a tendency to put on weight, both of which traits she passed on to me, one more welcome than the other. He was smitten. She was the daughter of a wealthy middle class Lwów family. Her father was the senior pharmacist for the Mikołasz pharmaceutical company in that city, while her mother was of Hungarian parentage.

That same year, happy flapper Ludmiła, only a little older than Władysław, met her future husband. Feliks Machnowski was a career soldier and a good one. Born in 1896, he was seven years older than Ludmiła but would have been vastly more experienced and worldly wise. In 1918 he had joined the Polish army and had fought during the Polish-Bolshevik war. He had already been awarded the Order of Virtuti Militari, Poland's highest military decoration for heroism and courage. This is the oldest military decoration in the world still in use, the equivalent of the British Victoria Cross. By 1922 he was promoted to captain and in November 1924 he was assigned to the Higher Military School in Warsaw for further training. Eligible scarcely begins to describe him and he must have been madly attractive to country born Ludmiła, who nevertheless shared her mother's romantic disposition and her liking for the finer things in life. The few people I've met who knew her always mentioned her good looks and fashion sense as well as her irrepressible sense of humour. When Anna Danuta's son wrote to me recently, one of the people he asked about was 'Ludmiła or Ludenka', wondering who she was and what had become of her, because his mother had spoken about her with such affection, as did my father. Given that Danuta was in her teens when Ludmiła was visiting Dziedziłów with her handsome husband, it's not hard to see what an impression this glamorous young stepsister must have made.

Feliks merits his own Wikipedia entry. A small picture of him in full dress uniform shows a solemn young man, with dark hair and the obligatory moustache, but there is a later, more informal snapshot, taken in June 1944, on the Croatian island of Haar, opposite the Italian Coast. This must have been after the battle for Monte Cassino, earlier that year, in which he had participated. But before that, there had been a harrowing war that included capture and deportation deep into the USSR, subsequent release to join General Anders' army, and a period as colonel in command of the evacuation centre in Tehran, to which many sick and weary Poles had travelled across the USSR after Stalin changed his mind and decided that it suited his interests better to join the Allies. The dictator released vast numbers of imprisoned Poles, clearly hoping that they would die on the journey. This 1944 image of Feliks shows a much more human, battle weary man, with dark eyes in a thin face, and the same high Slavic cheekbones as my father and grandfather.

When Ludmiła met him twenty years earlier, he was a young man, basking in the rewards of his own heroism, and they would have had no way of knowing what the future held for either of them. The army used to go on frequent manoeuvres in the countryside around Lwów, and the officers generally stayed in nearby country houses, so Ludmiła could have met him at Meryszczów or Dziedziłow but much more likely at some neighbouring mansion, like those belonging to the wealthy Potocki family. When I asked my father to write down his recollections of his childhood, and the family stories told about the time immediately before his birth, he remarked casually that the 'Potockis owned a lot of land around there'.

This was something of an understatement, as was the term 'country house'. The Potockis had been, and remained among the wealthiest and most powerful of all the families, not just of Galicia, but of the whole Austro-Hungarian empire. The Potocki Palace in Lwów – another beautiful butter yellow house – rivals Schönbrunn in Vienna in its opulence. In fact in the first part of the twentieth century, the family held some twenty-five percent of all the land of Galicia, including forty manor houses or palaces, large and small, scattered throughout the region. They would have hosted parties and balls, and there would have been many opportunities for the less overwhelmingly rich *szlachta* daughters to meet eligible young military men. Ludmiła and Feliks would have met at some social occasion and carried on the relationship via a string of similar entertainments interspersed with exciting trips to Warsaw for Ludmiła.

Later on, my father described both of them as charming and 'a lot of fun', an uncle and aunt who didn't take things too seriously, for all that Feliks had spent so much of his life in the army. Perhaps he liked to party hard when he wasn't fighting. In 1925, there are military 'permits to marry' in the Polska Zbrojna newspaper among whom are the names Feliks Zbigniew Machnowski and Ludvika Czerkawska. Soldiers could not marry without official permission. My father remembered hearing that the wedding had been in Warsaw, a big 'society' affair that had taken place the year before he was born, observing drily that Poland was 'more or less ruled by the colonels' at this time, so Ludka moved in high circles for a while, certainly in higher circles than the rest of the family, except for Anna, who could remember better times and had perhaps imbued her daughter with the expectation of privilege.

My grandparents also celebrated their wedding in 1925, at the Roman Catholic church in Jaryczów, and afterwards at their newly renovated house on the Dziedziłów estate. The whole village joined in the celebration and the feasting allegedly went on for three days. The wedding wasn't in the bride's home in Lwów, but Łucja's father died there in the same year, so perhaps he was already ailing and three day celebrations wouldn't have been appropriate.

It wasn't all fun and feasting, because in the same year, Anna Hanakowska died, aged fifty-four, probably at Feliksa. Her death certificate says that she died of heart disease, and she is buried, not at Meryszczów, but in the same grave as Uncle Julian, in the old cemetery at Dziedziłow, a sadly overgrown and unkempt place now. After Anna died and Władysław had taken over the estate at Dziedziłow, it became clear that Jan Hanakowski didn't have enough to do. Or perhaps he had too much to do, but not nearly enough independence in doing it. He was still estate manager, but I think the autonomy he had known during the first years of his marriage to Anna had gone, and once more, I find myself feeling a good deal of sympathy for him. What had happened to the ambitious young man with his love of dairy farming and ambitions as a cheesemaker? Effectively, he must have been sidelined, even though he carried on living at Feliksa, only a few kilometres from Dziedziłow itself. Presumably he had a little land of his own.

I turn to Google Maps to find a street view of the turning to this hamlet, now called Velyki Pidlyski, an enticing tree-fringed lane, down which I can't walk even though I long to do it, while a small brown dog that looks as though it may have come from there, waits to cross the road. There are photographs of the village on the site, an Orthodox church and a painted shrine, taken in May, all set amid that gorgeous light green of spring. There's one taken in February too, with snow on the ground, a study in whites and greys that looks as cold as it must have been, and makes me think of my father's tales of sleigh rides with his parents, in the moonlight.

Jan still worked on and for the estate. There was certainly plenty to be done. But I think Władysław breezily overrode many of his suggestions, not always advisedly. If middle brother Bogusław was, as my father always claimed, a better farmer than either of the others, Jan Hanakowski probably had more real expertise than any of them, but Władysław was determined to go his own way. When she grew older, Anna Danuta, went away to school, but she would come home for her holidays, especially in summer. After her mother's death in 1925, she spent at least some of her time with Władysław and his family on the main estate, which was understandable, since there would have been more female company and more excitement in the big house. It was hardly surprising that in due course, Jan remarried a local woman. I'm not certain of her name, but I recently received some photographs from one of Jan's grandsons, Roman, including a little snapshot of his mother, Danuta, with a very loving inscription to her father and what looks like the name Rosi, in all probability her stepmother. The couple had a son called Jerzy who, as I was later to discover, remembered my grandfather with a great deal of affection.

When Valeriy Podolynnyy, from Lviv, visited Dziedziłów, he told me that the first person he spoke to, in a village that seemed little changed, was an old man who also remembered my grandfather as a popular landowner.

'He tried hard to help the local people,' he said.

But then popularity doesn't always equate to competence. And once more, I remember how very young these people were, to have such responsibilities placed on their shoulders. I wonder how many of them may have had premonitions about what might be coming, an uneasiness about the future, based on their knowledge of the past, that made them seize the day, and make the most of life and love, wherever and whenever they could find it.

CHAPTER ELEVEN

Country Living and City Pleasures

I have three precious photographs of my grandfather. Two of them, I have known all my life, since they came through the war with my father, while I discovered the third in the book that Wanda Czerkawska's daughter Teresa wrote about her side of the family. The picture from Teresa's book is of the Czerkawski siblings at Meryszczów in 1926, very early in the year my father was born. Their mother, Anna, had died the previous year and 1925 was also the year that my grandfather took over his inheritance at Dziedziłow. Władysław is still wearing a black tie and a black armband, presumably for his mother and perhaps for his father-in-law as well. He is standing in the very centre of the picture, with the rest of the family arranged around him, and the focus is almost entirely on him, which is oddly touching. It feels as if he is looking straight out at me. Everyone else is slightly blurred. He looks thin, worried and absolutely worn out. The photograph seems to be an intrusion upon his privacy, his grief, and I can imagine him impatiently telling the photographer to 'get a move on'. His shoulders are slumped in exhaustion, he is wearing a crumpled and slightly baggy tweed suit, as though he has lost weight, and his arms are hanging resignedly down by his sides.

His sister, Wanda, then aged twenty-eight, is standing next to him, very close to him, and she's smiling, a little nervously. She may even have her arm threaded through his, although it's hard to tell. He was always her favourite. I don't think she has yet bobbed her hair, like the others, since it looks as though it is plaited, and tied up at the back. His wife, Łucja, is on the right. She's smiling too, and you can just make out the little bump of her pregnancy, because she's standing in profile, so in a sense, my father is in the picture too. There is a pretty young woman in pale clothes and a white cloche hat, just visible between Władysław and Łucja, who I think must be Ludmiła. Her family used the affectionate diminutives of Ludka or Ludenka, but in most official documentation, she's Ludwika or Ludovika, named for one of the Queens of Poland. Tall, good looking Zbigniew is on the right, at the very edge of the picture. On the left, a slightly smaller, but smart and self confident man stands, also in profile, his hands behind his back. I think he is Bogusław, and a tall lady at the back, also wearing a cloche hat, may be his wife, Niobcia. Somebody pointed out that she looks a little like me, and she does, but if she is Bogusław's wife, she is no blood relation. There is also a woman in some kind of uniform with a high, white, starched collar, who may have been the housekeeper. She is looking away from the family grouping, as though she doesn't quite belong and is faintly embarrassed to be there.

The next picture of my grandfather is a tiny head and shoulders image. This was badly damaged, having come through the war in my dad's various uniform pockets, but a photographer friend restored it for me. This time, he looks much more relaxed. He's wearing a neat collar and tie, and a jacket with some kind of ribbon in the lapel, probably leading down to the watch in his breast pocket. He's staring into the camera, and you can see that same widow's peak, the high cheekbones, long, straight nose, dark eyes, and a sensuous mouth. There is, when you look at the picture closely, just the hint of a smile and a gleam in his eyes, as though again, he's about to make some remark to the photographer, but this time it will be a joke. He can't resist it. I doubt if he would have been much more than twenty-six years old when it was taken, possibly even younger.

The third picture was taken a few years later, around 1929, when my father, Julian, was three or four years old. It's a family grouping, with Julian looking more like a little girl than a boy, as was the custom at that time. Boys 'went into trousers' later on. Dad has his hair in a short bob, he's wearing a light cotton smock that buttons down the front and you can just see that he has long white socks on his sturdy little legs, socks that probably wouldn't have stayed white for very long, since he was an active child. It's obviously summer, and the sun is shining, a very happy picture of a family threesome. Julian is standing behind a miniature 'tumbril' cart, a smaller example of the traditional horse drawn long carts you saw everywhere in rural Poland, even when I first went there in the 1970s, and which you probably still see to this day. This one has four wheels and a long handle so that Julek can haul it along. They are outside, somewhere on the estate, among shrubs and grasses, and the cart is full of cuttings. His mother is bending over, her hands resting on the cart for the benefit of the photographer, whoever he is. Some visiting family member perhaps? Łucja has a typical 1920s low-necked cotton or linen print dress, showing her cleavage as she bends forward. There are pearls around her neck, and the obligatory elegant cloche hat with a scarf at the side. She looks very happy. Just behind and between these two, my grandfather is bending forward too, with his hands on his knees, looking, as ever, slightly impatiently at the camera. On the back somebody, probably my grandmother, has written 'father, mother and Julian at Dziedziłow'. This was the beginning of the best of times for the family, a spell of loving peace before events within the family and in the world outside would bring terrible upheavals, and a tidal wave of destruction and misery.

My father was born in May 1926, a healthy time to be born, before the soft spring weather gave place to the heat of summer. As is usual with the places where we spend our early childhood, Dad could describe this place in great detail. He knew the old mansion house only as a ruin, with some of its cellars still intact, good places for an adventurous boy to play in. When the Russians burned the building, they had more or less left the gardens and orchards intact and some of the furnishings may even have been rescued and installed in the older house. Some of the surviving bricks from the mansion were later used in the construction of a new Roman Catholic church not far from the estate, a beautiful building that now, alas, also seems to have fallen into disrepair.

Władysław made good use of the old cellars to store apples and pears and other produce, and for his mushroom growing venture, one of several bright ideas he had for making money. Władysław was perennially short of ready money, but never short of ideas. He was always full of enthusiasm at the start of any venture, but easily bored, a trait I recognise all too clearly in myself. It is also difficult to separate my grandfather's tendency to early enthusiasms from the significant and growing problems caused by imminent political upheaval. I doubt if any of the inhabitants of Dziedziłow and Meryszczów, used to coping with the uncertainties and savagery of these disputed borderlands, could have predicted the full horror of what was to come. It says much for him that some of the older inhabitants of the village, and Jan Hanakowski's son by his second marriage, remembered him with such affection as a cheerful and generous young man.

In pride of place, in the centre of the park, was a three hundred year old linden tree, that had seen many successive monarchs and owners come and go. Whenever I smell that sweet, evocative scent of a linden in full bloom, invariably accompanied by the sound of bees, busy among the flowers, I think about my father and his love of lindens. To one side of the park was an orchard of apples and pears. It seems all very Chekhov, to us, now. Inevitably, there was a cherry orchard. But it was practical too. There was a market garden, where lettuces, peas and beans, cabbages and other root vegetables were grown. These were used for the house, but also sold on in large quantities. There were more gardens with soft fruit and many tomato plants. All these were a source of paid work and income for local people, but it was seasonal income and weather reliant. There were flower gardens around the house, with roses, dahlias and various annuals. The more formal gardens were closer to the ruins of the old mansion where they had been situated during Uncle Julian's residence, and they too had been restored, probably at more expense than was merited, but Władysław never liked to do things by halves. Besides, restoring what the Russians and other invaders had destroyed was de rigueur for the patriotic Pole, as it would be in the future.

There was what my father, in his written memoir, calls a pond, but at some two hundred yards long and seventy yards wide I would describe the existing stretch of water, if this is what he meant, as a lake. It was stocked with carp and fairly choked with reeds. The reeds are there still. They used to drain it from time to time and take the carp out to be sold. There was a little island covered in bushes, five meters from the shore. With a small boy's longing to explore, Julian had always nagged his father to take him there, so one day, Władysław did indeed take him over in a rowing boat but then, quite casually, left him there, wanting to see if he would have the initiative to get back. Julian must have been six or seven at the time. He described how, eventually, he waded across the narrowest part, which proved to be very shallow, and onto dry land again. Dad seemed fairly laid back about this experience, perhaps secure in the knowledge that his father would never abandon him completely, although he remembered that Łucja didn't approve of such treatment of her beloved son.

Around the feast of the Epiphany, on 6th January, there was an annual ceremony at the frozen pond. A big cross would be cut from the ice and raised up beside the lake.

There was a procession from the nearby Orthodox church and the priest held a service in the open air. Władysław, as the respected heir tenant, and a friend of the Ukrainian Orthodox priest, was expected to be present at the ceremony and to participate in it. There was a great crush of people, and almost every year somebody, sometimes more than one person, fell through the hole in the ice, and had to be hauled out, wrapped in blankets and revived with vodka. Later, in February, there were even harder frosts but only a little fresh snow by that time, and there was always skating on the pond with the old fashioned skates that you strapped onto your boots.

When he described this part of his childhood, my father listed exactly what he could remember of the many animals kept on the estate. There were four black trotting horses. These were dedicated carriage horses that could trot faster than the others could gallop, since galloping was ungainly (and very uncomfortable for passengers) in a carriage horse. There were three good riding horses of which the best was Władysław's stallion, Dzinnek. This thoroughbred and valuable horse was used to serve local mares, something my father remembered watching with 'great interest'. There were some forty sturdy farm horses, Polish *Koniks* that did most of the heavy hauling and ploughing. There was a herd of one hundred cows and twenty pigs, although this increased when Władysław planned to raise bacon for the English breakfast market. There was also a bull, kept for breeding purposes. Dad remembered plenty of cats, kept for controlling vermin on the farm, and several dogs, both pets and hunting animals. Wanda's future husband, artist Karol Kossak, later sketched a menagerie of domestic animals at Meryszczów, and it's not hard to imagine Dziedzilow being much the same. There were two Alsatian guard dogs called Bary and Nana, chained by day and loose by night, given that the attack on Uncle Julian would still be remembered and a repetition feared. There was also Baśka, a chocolate-coloured hunting dog, mainly Julian's pet and, he remembered, very fond of redcurrants. Many years later, Dad's Scottish rescue dog, called Bajka, another Polish doggy name meaning 'fairytale', also proved to be fond of redcurrants and bilberries, and became adept at picking them with her short front teeth. There were chickens, geese, ducks and guinea fowl, all of which were good to eat. A painting of Meryszczów from this time, shows a turkey, so these birds may have been kept for the table at Dziedziłow too. And of course there would have been plenty of eggs. Close to the house where the family now lived, there were tennis courts, paddocks, sheds, stables, a dairy, a farm store and a plum orchard that supplied the fruit for the plum dumplings that were my grandfather's favourite.

The first few years of my father's childhood were very happy. If there were tensions within the family, Julian wasn't yet aware of them. It was a privileged rural upbringing with affectionate parents, and he never lost his curiosity and his love of the countryside, even later on, when we were living in smoky Leeds. Weekends there often meant bus trips either to the moors at Ilkley and Bolton Abbey, or closer to home, to Cockersdale Woods, just outside Leeds, a bus ride along Whitehall Road where we lived until I was seven.

Cockersdale is still surprisingly rural, but it was unspoilt countryside back then. I remember his excitement when he first discovered a big pond with frogspawn. He showed me wasps' nests, a grass snake curled up in the sun, linden trees and mushrooms and wildflowers of all kinds. We had so many enchanting encounters with a natural world that must have been a cherished part of his own childhood. When, at my request, Dad wrote a detailed memoir of his early years in Dziedziłow, I understood why he had needed those excursions into the countryside and why, eventually, we moved to rural Ayrshire, where he must have felt even more at home. It suited my mother and myself as well. Mum may have been a city girl born and bred, but her forebears on both sides of her family had once been rural people too, and something of that love for the countryside lingered in her.

With the birth of his son, my grandfather, still only twenty-two years old, inventive and self-confident, came into his inheritance with more enthusiasm than experience, but with little inclination to admit to his shortcomings. In a laudable effort to make things work, not just for himself and his family but for those employed by the estate, he instituted all kinds of changes and innovations. Now you'd call it diversification and it should have worked, especially given the fact that there was a railway at nearby Zadwórze, and a massive potential market in the city of Lwów. He built a flour mill which must have been a blessing for the whole village, bred carp in the lake and started a hundred hive apiary. He grew tomatoes for the Lwów market, until one spring they lost five thousand plants to frost, which dampened his enthusiasm somewhat. As well as raising pigs for the British bacon market, fired by his enthusiasm for a Britain he had never seen, he tried growing mushrooms in the ruined cellars of the big yellow house, without notable success. There were more and better mushrooms in the forests around the estate.

He taught himself English, purely out of interest, to a standard where he could read books in that language, a skill that he tried to pass on to his son, one which would come in very handy for Julian in ways that his father could never have imagined, even in his worst nightmares. He was a good shot, but he also loved to play chess. He was, of course, an excellent horseman. Even though this was peacetime, albeit a fragile peace that could be shattered at any moment, he was from a long line of cavalrymen. He would still have proudly called himself a lancer, and this heritage and these skills would never be forgotten.

Perhaps his most serious passion, though, was for cars. He bought the first and indeed the only car in the district, a powerful, six-cylinder Chrysler Open Top Tourer from America. It cost 100,000 zloty, about £3000 in 1930, a huge sum of money. Where did he get the money? Presumably from his inheritance that might have been better spent on the estate. Where did he learn to drive? I've no idea. It was probably the only car within a radius of fifty miles. The top speed was an impressive 112 kilometres per hour, but on the poor roads of Galicia, this was rarely if ever achieved. I doubt if this would have prevented Władysław from trying. The tyres were poor and even a fairly short trip to the city resulted in frequent punctures. Łucja rarely drove, although her enthusiastic husband encouraged her to try. When she did, Julian remembered that there were occasional accidents. On one trip, the car landed in a ditch. 'I was in the back and found myself suddenly sitting on top of a trunk in a field!' says dad. Fortunately, he was unharmed. 'On another occasion, in Gdynia, my mother ran over a policeman's foot.' Family history is silent as to the consequences of this accident, especially for the poor policeman. Driving tests were introduced in the UK in the 1930s, but in an area where cars were still few and far between, people like Władysław probably learned from friends and by a combination of trial and error. There is a photograph of Julian behind the wheel of that splendid car, at Dziedziłow, aged five, according to the date of 1931 on the back of the picture. He's wearing a motoring hat and goggles, and holding onto the steering wheel in fierce concentration. The car is in focus, but the slightly blurred trees behind him are in full leaf and there is a long, low building in the distance. Did Władysław actually let him drive on the estate? I expect he did.

There was an important race circuit in Lwów, and Władysław would sometimes take his son to see the racing there, perhaps dreaming that one day he would be involved in the sport. It's difficult for us now to conjure up the novelty and glamour of motor racing at that time. These visits were intensely exciting for young Julian, with the opportunity to see so many cars at close quarters, while his father chatted in English to the foreign drivers, including the famous Rudolf Caraciolla, a descendent of Italian migrants to Germany. There was a 'Wedel' Viennese café in Lwów, an authentic Viennese pastrycook, with luscious chocolate cakes and large marzipan and cream concoctions in various shapes and sizes. The visits to Lwów always involved an hour or so there for father and son, before heading home. Władysław, indulgent as ever, let Julian eat two or three of these rich cakes at once, and he was sometimes sick on the way home, although they agreed that it would be wiser not to tell his mother what had happened.

Less easy to hide was the time Władysław broke his nose on the way back to Dziedziłow after another trip to Lwów. As usual on these roads, he had a puncture. Repairing it meant taking the wheel off and removing the tyre, first taking off the round piece of metal holding it in place. He was enthusiastically digging this out with a jemmy when it sprang up, hitting him straight across his nose. Julian admired the way his father still managed to drive the car home in his somewhat battered and bloody state. Jan Hanakowski's son, Jerzy, wrote to me that when he was a little boy of four or five, Władysław would often give him a ride back to Feliksa in the car, a pleasure that he had remembered his whole life. A kindly man then, full of good humour.

Later, my father reflected that he probably had far too much money for such a young man with significant responsibilities. Władysław's cash must have come with the inheritance, money that should have been put straight back into the estate, but although he worked hard, he squandered money too. When something interested him, as with motor sport, he would put all his energy into it and spend far more than was wise. When he tired of it, he would turn his attention elsewhere. He worked hard and played hard and he was something of a Casanova, flirting outrageously when the occasion arose.

Sometimes, he did a lot more than flirt.

Several children in the village, said my father, were nick-named 'young master'. Those using the term would do so with a nod and a wink. Moreover, the children looked like Władysław. He didn't deny them. Any woman involved would be given a gift of some acres of land. Land was at a premium. This in turn meant that the woman in question would have suitors, in spite of her pregnancy, and the child would generally be accepted as the bringer of good fortune it undoubtedly was. Pondering on this as a happily married adult, my father remarked that his mother seemed to accept this state of affairs more or less without complaint for a time. I can say with absolute certainty that my mother wouldn't have accepted it at all, not for a moment, even if my father had been so inclined, but then the world was changing for that generation too, he had seen enough excitement to last a lifetime and he loved my mother till the day he died. From what I can gather, my grandfather's interests in almost everything, including his romances, were sudden, intense but short lived. Comparisons with Toad of Toad Hall, albeit considerably better looking, are irresistible. On the other hand, land was exactly what the smooth running of the estate needed, and slowly but surely some of it seems to have leached away, not just as a sweet-ener for favours rendered, but in an effort to raise more money for various new projects, all-consuming when first mooted, less so as time passed.

One example of these illicit relationships and their complexities involved Julian's nanny, Marynia. It is also an example of the considerable difficulties I've had in writing this book, simply because the tapestry is almost too rich, so much so that you have to stare at it for a long time before the finer details become clear. Marynia's parents had a smallholding at the end of the village and were not particularly well off, but they did have a little land of their own and a certain status in the community. They were Polish, and Marynia's father was both patriotic and very religious. One quirk of his character was an intense dislike of cats, but the priest's cat often wandered into the new church beside the village, perhaps drawn by the warmth, and perhaps to keep the inevitable mice in check. Marynia's father could be seen praying fervently and ostentatiously at Sunday Mass. The cat, as cats unerringly do single out those who dislike them, would walk along the bench towards him and he would pause in his praying to curse the animal volubly, before resuming his dialogue with the Almighty, incidentally causing great amusement among the rest of the congregation, especially the children.

Marynia was a confident young woman, with long blonde hair that she always plaited and coiled up on her head in the traditional way. Her mother had the same long plaited hair. In winter, she wore a headscarf, several skirts for warmth, and a big sheepskin coat and boots. By contrast, Dad always pictured Marynia in summer, with her corn coloured hair and her prettily embroidered blouses and skirts. Until Julian was seven, when he started school, Marynia would come in daily to look after him, spending the whole day in the house

Julian loved his nanny very much, and I think she loved him. She did the ironing and told him fairy tales and ghost stories while she worked, traditional tales, with 'plenty of murder and mutilation' he wrote. She would use a charcoal iron, probably the oldest form of iron in existence. This was a shaped metal box with holes in it, a hinged lid and a flat plate on the bottom for smoothing the fabric. You would fill it with hot coals from the range. It had a wooden handle on the top, so that the person doing the ironing didn't burn her fingers, but it did have a tendency to leave black specs on white linens. Dad remembered that once the hot coals were introduced into the 'box', his nanny would wave it about, to heat up the plate. It produced plenty of carbon monoxide, so the storytelling sessions would always give Julian a fearsome headache but it seemed worth it for the pleasure of the stories and Marynia's company.

She had a daughter who was a couple of years younger than Julian, a child called Paulina (or possibly Polina) who would often accompany her mother to the house. As they grew a little older, the two children were on good terms and played together. Paulina had the characteristic dark good looks of the Czerkawskis and was almost certainly Julian's step-sister. Estate workers would say 'what a nice girlfriend Paulina would make for you, Julek!' while little Julian had no idea why they found this notion so funny. It was only much later that he became aware of the relationship.

Marynia, however, had a boyfriend in the village, also a young man with dark good looks. He was a clever, taciturn Ukrainian – a passionate Bolshevik – called Józef Szwagulak, who worked on the estate farm. He had jet black hair and sharp features, and he was an excellent dancer. He could dance the sexy and energetic *hopak*, and Julian remembered him dancing with his mother, Łucja, at some estate celebration and how much his mother enjoyed it. An attractive man, for sure, but one with few means at his disposal. And he had no land at all. Certainly he wouldn't have been rich or even solvent enough for Marynia's father to agree to any marriage between a Ukrainian and a Pole. Patriotic principles tended to dissolve in the face of prosperity or status but Jósef had neither.

Marynia's father disliked my grandfather intensely, probably because of Paulina, but wasn't much fonder of Jósef either. He must have wondered why his daughter couldn't find herself a 'nice young Pole' to marry. However, after the birth of Paulina, and while she continued to look after Julian and her own child during the day, Władysław gave Marynia a decent parcel of land, which meant that she could marry whomever she liked and she seemed to like Jósef very much indeed. At this point, Jósef too was helpfully presented with some land of his own. Much as he might disapprove, there was nothing that Marynia's father could do or say about it, and it was certainly a good deal for the young couple and their family. Whatever he thought of Władysław, Jósef and Marynia remained very fond of Julian, a fondness that was to be called on when Julian was in his teens and urgently needed their help.

CHAPTER TWELVE

The Amazon and the Artist

In 1974, I visited Poland for the first time, and spent several weeks with my great aunt Wanda and my great uncle Karol Kossak, from a family of distinguished Polish artists, in their apartment in Ciechocinek, a spa town to the north west of Warsaw. I went by ferry and by train from Rotterdam to Warsaw, travelling across Europe without benefit of a sleeper because I couldn't afford one, dozing in my seat whenever I could. I became so tired that when I closed my eyes, my brain began to translate the multitude of foreign voices around me into a bizarre kind of English. It was the experience of a lifetime, although not always in a good way. But it did give me some tiny inkling of what my grandfather and other members of his family had suffered on those terrible wartime train journeys, or worse, treks on foot across the Soviet Union. I was warm, well fed and well clothed. They were sick, starving and full of despair.

It was exhausting.

The journey was a long one, even though I was ensconced in a reasonably comfortable seat on a reliable train, with food and hot drinks arriving every so often, depending on which country we happened to be passing through. The border crossing at Marienborn loomed. I became aware of a certain tension on the train. Cheerful Polish people who had been laughing and singing became quiet and thoughtful. It would be even worse on the way back, but by then I knew the form and would be mentally prepared for it, secure in the knowledge that I had a British passport. This was the old crossing from West to East Germany, and it was hideous. It was night time when the train drew to a halt, with a great creaking of brakes and residual hisses and groans. It must, by then, have been a big diesel locomotive but for me, it felt as though I was in an old movie.

It was hard to see what was happening outside, but there were flashlights, footsteps and the tension on the train became palpable. I have never known such an acute sense of danger. Unsmiling men in grey uniforms, men bristling with weapons, clambered aboard, slamming doors behind them. They had dogs, fierce German Shepherds. They checked everything and everybody. They looked under the seats and in the luggage racks. I handed over my passport, nervously, because the fear was contagious. My sense of my own powerlessness in the face of very real danger has stayed with me. I needn't have worried, because the official, pale faced in a grey uniform, glanced at it, glanced at me, handed it back and moved on without another word. It struck me afterwards that he looked weary beyond belief, just so damned tired of it all. Other people were not so lucky. There were arguments, shouting, general rudeness, endless suspicion. People being treated as guilty of something, anything. Much the same thing happened later on in our journey when we traversed Berlin, crossing the border from West to East Berlin, passing through stations that made me think of spy novels. Years later, reading China Miéville's *The City & The City*, a novel that takes that sense of a city at war with itself to illuminating extremes, I remembered that experience. In 1989, when I found myself in tears at the fall of the Berlin Wall, I thought about that train trip all over again, and over the ensuing decades marvelled at how Germany has managed to navigate these terrifying waters, greatly assisted by the ideals of the EU.

It was a relief to arrive in Poland. The name on my passport even elicited a smile from the border guard there. I took another train to Ciechocinek, where Wanda and Karol had lived since 1948, arriving in this attractive spa town in late summer sunshine. I remember most of all, their welcome for me, a stranger, and their kindness. Karol was seventy-eight by then, and Wanda the same age. He was an artist from a family of celebrated Polish painters, tall and charming. She was as active as a chaffinch, a pretty woman, her soft grey hair coiled up on top of her head, her clothes neat and smart, and she was obviously still in love with him.

'My sunshine,' she called him.

Their belongings, including a large piano and pictures, some by Karol himself and a few by his illustrious forebears, were crammed into a shabby apartment on the ground floor of what must once have been a comfortable town house, divided into smaller units by the post war Stalinist government. There were two rooms and a tiny bathroom. The room in which they cooked and ate, and in which I slept on an upholstered bench, was at the back of the house, facing onto a veranda and a garden, which gave them some extra space in summer. The room at the front of the house was where Karol still painted, although his eyesight was failing. It was where he played the piano, and where they slept. It was cramped but comfortable. To me, it felt very foreign, very Polish. There were bright woven hangings tacked to the walls behind the fitted seating, softening them. There was a fringed cloth on the table that sat under the main light. Wanda always placed a little vase of fresh flowers from the garden in the middle.

Every night, Wanda sat at the table, reading, embroidering or mending. She gave me the impression of being handy in all kinds of ways: sewing, baking, preserving garden produce. Karol would sketch or write letters, his handwriting a scrawl, because his sight was failing. But his art was still, as it had been all his life, his mode of expressing himself and that never seemed to fail him, no matter how hard he found it to see clearly. He was always, he said, being asked to paint 'jolly Hucul weddings'. These were watercolours of traditional mountain wedding scenes, with the bride and groom in picturesque costumes, and he hated them. Unfortunately, people still wanted them, and the couple needed the money they brought in. I think he had started painting them when he and Wanda were living in the Carpathian mountains at Tatarów, an old village on the beautiful river Prut, but their success had become a burden. Still, he would paint them to commission, swearing gently to himself.

'*Cholera*! *Psia krew*!' he would mutter. 'Cholera, dog's blood!' while Wanda tutted disapprovingly.

There was an old fashioned wireless in the living room, and I sat with them, listening to Chopin's First Piano Concerto broadcast from Warsaw, with moths blundering around the light, both light and music fluctuating occasionally because of the uncertain power supply. Whenever I hear that music now, I'm back there, sitting with them, enchanted by them.

Wanda baked gingerbread for me. She fed me homemade cheese, soft and white, honey from a neighbour who kept bees, fresh rye bread with caraway seeds, and plums from the overgrown garden. I didn't know then that she had once kept bees herself, when she was the main breadwinner of her little family. Karol charmed me. He took me walking round the town, kissed my hand in the traditional way, bought me coffee and cognac in a succession of cafés and sketched on paper napkins for me: keen caricatures of the privileged party members who came to the spa to take the waters, as well as *chochliks*, bizarre ghouls and goblins, often satirically conflating the two. I have them still. Sometimes we would walk into the countryside around the town. We would go arm in arm, in the evening, when a mist spread over the flat fields and women were burning the last of the potato leaves. I wrote a poem about those evenings. 'Though I hurtle through youth for love of him, he's gone too far before,' I wrote. And it did feel like that. I just wished I had known both of them when they were younger. My grandfather too.

The town had horse drawn *dorożki* (droshkys) instead of taxis and all the drivers saluted him as he passed by. He examined the horses and offered praise or advice or criticism, which the drivers accepted without complaint. The Kossaks were known for their equine studies and their expertise. Cruelty was unthinkable in his presence. Karol was the grandson of Juliusz and the nephew of Wojciech Kossak, both of them Polish artists whose canvases still fetch record prices at auction. My Polish was limited, as was their English, so we spoke in French and muddled through pretty well. He told me about the old days in Lwów and Dziedziłow, and especially about my grandfather, who had been his good friend, back when they were young and hopeful.

Even then, young as I was, I could see that Wanda and Karol were a relic of a world that was long gone, preserved in the amber sunshine of small town Poland. Years later, when I saw a production of The Merry Widow in Vienna, I wondered why Count Danilo seemed so familiar. He reminded me of Karol. I still miss him. He died the following year. By that stage I was working in Finland, but I travelled across the Baltic to spend Christmas with my Polish family in Warsaw. We went to Ciechocinek and visited the cemetery where he is buried, and lit candles for him, amid snow flurries that threatened to extinguish them, but I couldn't imagine the long, brave, elegant length of him down there, no matter how hard I tried. My cousin told me that at his funeral, all the *dorożki* in Ciechocinek drove in procession, following his cortege. Wanda lived on till 1983, and I met her again, spending another Christmas with her when I was sponsored by the British Council to teach English at Wrocław University. That was a Christmas during which the family introduced me to numerous remote relatives, all anxious to place me in the annals of the family – Julian's daughter, Władysław's grand-daughter, Wanda and Karol's niece. I was being accorded my place, in the nicest possible way. No getting away from it. That was who I was.

As a young woman Wanda seems to have been overshadowed by her vibrantly pretty sister, but it was through Ludmiła that she met her future husband and the love of her life. One of Karol's younger sisters, probably Anna, had been at boarding school with Ludmiła. In summer, Ludka liked to host house parties of young people at Meryszczów. Wanda was the quieter of the two sisters but popular with their friends. A few years earlier she had been fascinated by a young Austrian officer, who enjoyed painting. Teresa didn't seem to know his name, and Wanda wasn't telling, but neither his portrait nor his work survived in the family annals. All the same, Wanda's fondness for artists persisted. There had been some fear in the family that, at the advanced age of twenty-seven, this quiet young woman was in danger of becoming an 'old maid' which was unacceptable in those more traditional times. What were unmarried women to do? Her beloved younger brother was already married and in possession of his estate at Dziedziłow, so her only alternative was to stay at Meryszczów, with the eldest, Zbigniew, and keep house for him there. I don't think Zbigniew was too keen on that option, and neither was she, but it would have been the only one available to her.

In 1925 a young painter called Karol Kossak accompanied his sister to Meryszczów for one of those big summer parties that the *szlachta* still enjoyed. Karol was almost thirty by that time, and Ludmiła and Anna may have been doing a little matchmaking between them. A few years earlier, he had been much more interested in the pretty younger sister herself, but then she had met Feliks Machnowski. Against such a military hero, a poor artist didn't stand a chance. In spite of the celebrity of his fore-bears, there didn't seem to be much disposable money in the Kossak coffers either.

In 1925, the year when Władysław married my grand-mother and Ludka married her Feliks, Karol suddenly noticed the quiet elder sister. Wanda was not wealthy, but the old name and the *szlachta* status stood for a lot. As a young man, Karol had fought in the First World War, having been drafted into the Austrian Army, until he was badly wounded at the Italian Front and sent home. That had been almost ten years previously, but there was a certain vulner-ability about him. He seemed to need looking after, said his daughter, and Wanda had been looking after demanding people since she was a child. She was captivated by Karol. Even in his late seventies, the full blast of his old fashioned charm was devastating. There are a few photographs of him from the 1920s, seated at an easel or on picnics with groups of young people. I'm looking at one taken in 1926, at *Górki* Wielkie in Silesia, with his close cousin Zofia Kossak, a writer who was to become a resistance fighter in WWII. In 1942, Zofia wrote bravely about the Warsaw Ghetto. 'All will perish, poor and rich, old, women, men, youngsters, infants. Their only guilt is that they were born into the Jewish nation condemned to extermination by Hitler.' She added that the world was silent in the face of the atrocity. Even those who were fighting against the toxic Nazi dogma. She was arrested, and sent to Auschwitz, but when the Nazis realised who she was, she was sent back to Warsaw to be interrogated and publicly executed as an example to others. Through the efforts of the Polish resistance, she was released in 1944, and defiantly participated in the Warsaw Uprising. She lived until 1968, she was recognised in Jerusalem as one of the 'righteous among the nations' and was posthumously awarded the highest Polish honour, the Order of the White Eagle. But all that was in the future for this happily oblivious picnic party. Her husband is sitting on the left of the picture, pouring drinks from a small flask, possibly alcoholic drinks or coffee, from the small size of the metal cups. Karol is seated at the back, with a pretty girl on either side of him.

I always think of him as tall, and he was, but in those 1926 pictures he was slender and fragile, the very picture of the needy artist. His wartime experiences had matured him and given him a keen perception of human evil, a perception that often emerged in his more satirical sketches and paintings. Physically, at that time, he seemed boyish. He was a fine watercolourist, but never had quite the celebrity of his forebears, Juliusz and Wojciech. Nevertheless, he was welcomed at Meryszczów and started to visit there more often, painting small landscapes of the country round about and even the entrance to the house itself. Two of these watercolour sketches, printed in his daughter's memoir of the family, are particularly intriguing, since they give a good sense of the estate as it was back then: impressive, a little untidy but full of life and growth. One of them shows a pair of imposing white painted stone gateposts, with heavy wooden gates propped open and a vague impression of buildings behind them. A turkey struts in the foreground. In another, chickens peck beneath the trees. There's a driveway and a white building, with mature trees in the foreground. I wish he had painted the whole house. Maybe he did, and maybe the image didn't survive. He was fond of sketching horses and dogs, but in particular, he loved to paint Wanda, straight and striking, astride a horse, no side saddle for her, a picture he titled 'Wanda, the Amazon'. I think he admired her as a horsewoman before ever he admired her as a woman. She looked good on a horse. Her posture was good and her equestrian skills far surpassed those of her friends, but she was a well educated, well read young woman who appreciated the arts. The more he got to know her, the more he liked her sheer 'unaffectedness' as her daughter termed it. Wanda was never a flirt. She just liked him, and wasn't afraid to show it.

There was one problem. He was, according to the family, a 'holysz' – somebody with no means. And you didn't marry into a szlachta family without means. Or not without risking disapproval, as Anna had found more than a decade earlier when she married Jan. Fortunately for Karol, he received a commission to paint two portraits of Arab racehorses from the breeding stables of the late Prince Roman Sanguszko, in Gumniska. When I looked up Gumniska and racehorses, the first entry on Google showed a picture of Arabian horses by Karol's grandfather, Juliusz, so the family name, coupled with Karol's talents as an equestrian artist, would have helped. It was a commission with a deadline. He hated deadlines, but he took it, and proposed to Wanda on the proceeds. Not only that, but such a high profile commission meant that he was suddenly a young man with prospects. He and Wanda were married in October 1927 in the parish church in nearby Przemyślany.

Some of the wedding gifts sound quite sumptuous: a silver cutlery set for twenty-four people and a solid silver tray, a fine leather suitcase, a Singer sewing machine from her sister (highly desirable and very expensive back then). More prosaically, there was a 'porcelain scrubbing board', sets of wool duvets and bed-covers. There were also two small paintings by Juliusz Kossak, which were probably the most precious gifts of the lot.

The marriage of a noblewoman to an artist from such a notoriously 'bohemian' family of artists, writers and similar ne'er-do-wells, was not welcomed by the whole family, but my grandfather and Karol soon became close friends. I think they were all relieved to see Wanda finally settled. Besides, Anna was no longer around to be hypocritically indignant. Many years later, Wanda was told by some distant relative that her father had actually written in his will that no daughter of his should ever marry 'a foreigner, an artist, a lousy lawyer or a soldier'. I don't know what my great grandfather had against lawyers, but one daughter married a soldier and one an artist, while his grandson went on to marry a foreigner, my mother. Perhaps the prejudice against artists in particular was related to some lingering resentment against Wyspiański and his wife's early fondness for him.

After the wedding, with Zbigniew in sole possession of Meryszczów, the couple lived at Jakimów, on a small-holding with a few acres of garden and land not far from Dziedziłów. Karol and Władysław were close friends, and Władysław was his wife's favourite brother, so it seemed like a happy arrangement. Karol was not nearly as practical as Wanda, and it was she who tended to the flower and vegetable gardens including growing vegetables to eat and to sell, since Karol's income was and would remain precarious.

'I remember them growing beans. Lots of beans,' said my father.

The Dziedziłow estate comprised several other villages. The small estate at Koniuch, given to Bogusław and Niobcia, Feliksa where Jan Hanakowski lived, and the house and garden given to Wanda and Karol would all have been part of Władysław's inheritance from Uncle Julian. The land belonging to the estate consisted of fields, meadows and woodland. There were some very poor cottages, but apart from the usual local trades, such as the blacksmith, the village mainly comprised what we would describe as smallholdings, each one a small farm with its own gardens and strips of land. It looked like a village from the distance but the closer you came, the more scattered it seemed. During Władysław's time, too much of the land belonging to the estate, land that Uncle Julian had treasured, was sold off and it seemed less viable with every year that passed. It would be hard to say whether this was down to Władysław's incompetence, his uneasy relationship with his farm manager, or the general and growing difficulties experienced by Galicia in those years between the wars. The terrible turbulence of WWI and earlier may have subsided but unrest or the threat of it ran like a background to all their ventures.

CHAPTER THIRTEEN

My Beloved Little Julian

The house at Dziedziłow was comfortable and, for the time, convenient. As with the other family houses, only half was two full storeys high and the bedrooms were all in the new extension. The old part was bigger than the new but it had an enormous attic. The downstairs rooms were connected by double doors in the manner of many Central and Eastern European houses. As a child, Julian couldn't remember being aware of the doors, but he thought that most of them had probably been propped open all the time. The interior was full of pictures by Karol Kossak and other artists, especially pictures of horses, and Karol's typical sketches of grotesque woodland creatures that greatly appealed to his brother-in-law's sense of humour. Władysław painted too, though he found it very hard to finish anything, something that seems to have been a besetting sin with him throughout his short life. His little son had much more application and was happy to paint with his Uncle Karol.

Kelim carpets softened the walls of various rooms, just as so many years later, the Kossaks still decorated the walls of their apartment in Ciechocinek with textiles. There was a little ante room leading into the dining room, and it was there that Władysław liked to nap after lunch, stretching himself out on a big ottoman, comfortably ensconced with piles of cushions, pulling the lower edge of the wall carpet over himself to make a kind of tent. His little son was always getting into trouble for rushing about on the parquet floors and making a noise while his father was thus engaged. However, he wasn't the only one. There were rugs and carpets in plenty on these highly polished floors and Karol and Władysław would occasionally chase Julian, and sometimes each other round the house from sheer exuberance. One day, Karol went head over heels when a rug slid along the polished floor and took the feet from under him. He always carried a fine tape measure in his pocket and on this occasion he pulled it out, pretending for his little nephew's benefit that the tendon was coming out of his leg.

Julian's memories of this house and its inhabitants are – like Wanda's of Meryszczów – very vivid. Every room in the house had a large tiled stove. This was filled up each morning with a basket of well seasoned logs from the forest and would then would burn for hours. The tiled stove setter travelled about from village to village, installing and repairing these stoves. Even in less affluent houses, they looked like small but efficient works of art. The Dziedziłow house, large as it was, must have been very warm in winter. There was no wallpaper, but the walls were plastered and some of them were stencilled. Julian's room in particular, was painted in various rainbow bands of colour, to his father's design. The one thing in his life that Władysław never grew bored with, never lost interest in, was his son.

There was already electricity in the house when Julian was a boy, installed during the renovation, so there were lamps in the rooms and even a couple of candelabra. The power came from the flour mill, where a generator had

been installed, mostly for the benefit of the milling process but of benefit to the house as well. If the mill had to
stop for some reason, the engineer would flick the lights
three times, and then wait five minutes before throwing
the switch, so that the family had time to light the big oil
lamps, still kept all over the house. There was no mains
water, but the water was pumped into the house in some
way because there was a flush toilet and a bathroom
upstairs, with a large porcelain bath, for which the water
took a long time to heat. In the kitchen there was a range
for cooking. The only fuel used in this and in the various
stoves was hard wood such as beech from the forest, never
soft, which would burn away in no time.

This was a pleasantly cluttered house. There were orna-
ments, painted cabinets full of porcelain and silver, and
sculptures in wood and marble. There was a silver samovar,
which wasn't used nearly as often as the one at Meryszczów
where Anna's husband had been so fond of his tea. There
was a piano but I'm not sure if either of my grandparents
played it. I learned when I was a child and progressed quite
far, stopping my lessons when I went off to university and
resuming them later. I still play, still have a battered copy
of Für Elise, with one of my dad's cartoons sketched on it.
He's on his knees, begging me to play it, while my young
self, looking like Tove Jansson's Little My, is turning her
nose up at him. Now when I'm playing, it strikes me that
perhaps Władysław could play. Certainly Uncle Karol, who
was a frequent visitor to the house, would have taken full
advantage of it, playing Chopin, Mozart and Beethoven for
the family and for his own pleasure.

Some of the possessions that filled the rooms may have been rescued from the pancake yellow manor house, while some would have come as wedding gifts from affluent friends. The dining room cutlery was solid silver, and there was a full Polish dinner service in blue and white porcelain with fine gilding. Władysław's most treasured indoor possession was his enormous home-made radio, with an aerial made of very thin wire, wound around the frame, and with batteries and accumulators. Julian was often accused of dislodging this aerial but he was intrigued by the contraption. Father and son loved gadgets and Dad never lost his fascination for tinkering about with technology, so he probably had been guilty of dislodging the aerial.

In the dining room there was a finely carved oak table, made by a local craftsman. There were twelve chairs, all with matching carvings, a carved oak sideboard and a small cabinet. When Julian was very young and his Aunt Danuta was in her teens, she used to get up at night and raid this cabinet for any food that had been left over from dinner, sometimes sharing it with him in late night bedroom picnics.

One of these downstairs rooms was used by Władysław as a library and study, with books bound in calf skin. There was a set of Polish classics by Bolesław Prus, (the pseudonym of Aleksander Głowacki) there were inevitably books by Wyspiański, as well as modernist writer and four times Nobel prize nominee Stefan Żeromski. Władysław's reading was nothing if not eclectic. It was here that he was always trying to invent a 'perpetuum mobile' machine, drawing endless diagrams and even attempting to construct it. As my scientist father pointed out later, a little sadly, it isn't possible. But maybe Władysław didn't know or maybe he simply didn't believe it and thought he might make all their fortunes if he could do it. For me, there is something very Polish about this: the insistence that the impossible might well be possible, if only you can find the right way of going about it. Looking at Warsaw's beautifully restored post war Old Town, it strikes me that sometimes they even manage it. I'm sure Ukraine will manage to achieve the same restoration in due course.

In spite of Władysław's occasional peccadilloes, there followed some reasonably happy years for the little family at Dziedziłow, even though no more children were born to Łucja and her husband. Once again, I can track these years through a few snapshots from that time, taken by Władysław, pictures he developed in his own dark room.

The earliest of these is a snapshot of Julian, perched on a rocking horse. The horse has an elongated face, a bridle and saddle and a long, silky mane and was probably made on the estate. I think he's in his parents' room rather than his own. He's very small, no more than two years old, with dark bobbed hair, the chubby cheeks and starfish fingers of a young child, and he's wearing a pinafore, to which he remembered that he strongly objected. The photograph has suffered from its long, troubled journey to England. There are creases and fingerprints, although these are probably from its original rather careless developer, my grandfather himself, who enjoyed dabbling in photography as well as so much else. There's a light above Julian, and the horse is in front of a large wardrobe with a mirror. You can make out a hat box on top of it, and possibly a very fancy hat beside it. Some of this elusive room is reflected in the wardrobe mirror behind him. You can see his bobbed hair, the cross-over straps of the pinafore, the heartrending vulnerability of a small child. Later, he would have tin toy motor cars, a bicycle, a wooden cart for pulling along, sleighs and skis.

There was an attic above the oldest part of the house, cram full of fascinating things. Most of these had been stored there since well before the yellow mansion had been built, so they would have belonged to the previous owners of the estate at a time when this house was still the main dwelling. There were cavalry sabres, flintlock pistols, chests full of old clothes in the fashions of distant times, and all kinds of things stacked against the walls: broken chairs, ancient wooden furniture, half finished pictures. Many of these pictures were Władysław's impatient attempts at emulating his more talented brother-in-law. Julian liked to go up and rummage in there, finding all kinds of things to marvel at. In this same attic was a door that led into a smaller room. You ventured through the door, and there was a single enormous chimney, into which the smoke from all the other stoves in the house was fed. This was used for smoking salami, sausages and hams, and must have smelled wonderful.

The bedrooms were in the newer part of the house. Danuta had her own room here. Zbigniew often came from Meryszczów and Łucja's sister Nusia visited from Lwów. The Czerkawskis had other guests to stay for quite long periods, but not in this house. There were guest cottages in the grounds where they lodged, joining the family for meals. There was a cook, the most highly paid of all the female employees, who lived somewhere on the estate and came in daily. On washdays, two women came from the village to do the heavy work. The laundry was one of a number of utility buildings, out of sight of the main house, accessed through the orchard. The washing was boiled in a copper, just as it was in my grandmother's infinitely smaller house in industrial Leeds. Since there were always visitors, there was plenty of washing. Bedlinen was put through an enormous box mangle, consisting of a trough, and a box with stones on rollers. This would press the fibres of the linen back into shape. The linen banqueting tablecloths and sheets were stored on wooden rollers to stop them from getting too creased. Besides the cook and kitchen help there were two maids, a butler who lived in his own cottage on the estate, and many other staff, farm workers as well as stable hands. Essentially, the estate was the main source of employment in the village.

Early breakfast in the house consisted of bread rolls, coffee, tea or milk and various preserves made with fruit from the garden. At mid morning, there might be a sandwich, usually with meat, especially for those who had been up and about early in the morning. The main meal of the day was a large, late lunch at one or two o'clock. This consisted of soup, which in summer might be apple or some other sweet 'fruit soup', a main course of meat, game or fish, with compote or a fruit pudding for dessert. Julian refused to eat the typically Polish fruit soups and had an abiding memory of disliking them very much. At night, there would be a supper of bread, cheese and cured meats. It sounds as though this timetable was still organised around a traditionally heavy working day with early starts and the need for snacks.

When Julian was hungry between meals, he went to see the cook, whom he always addressed as 'Pani' – my lady. He remarked that he was taught to be respectful to adults at all times. His father would tolerate nothing else. All the bread was home made, and he was allowed to play with the big flat shovels from the baking ovens and to take the bread out when it was baked. The cook would cut him a thick slice of fresh bread, upon which she poured a good helping of cream, sprinkling plenty of brown sugar on top. It was a precarious snack, he said, one that you had to lick all round as you ran off with it, to catch the delicious dripping cream. On one occasion, when the usual snack hadn't been forthcoming, Julian decided to sample the resin from the plum trees in the nearby orchard and discovered that it made him very sick indeed.

After the picture of Julian on his rocking horse, comes the family trio in the garden, taken around 1929 when Julian was three years old. The Czerkawskis were a sociable couple, and throughout this whole time, there were plenty of visitors. There would be tennis parties in summer, fishing parties at the river and lake, and a great many picnics. Poles seem to have been as fond of their picnics as any other nation. There were bridge parties, as well as theatre and concert visits to Lwów, some 40 kilometres away, by train or even by car, although if they went to evening events, they spent the night in the city. Old Uncle Julian had kept an apartment in the city, and Władysław may have retained the tenancy for his family. Sometimes they took Julian, sometimes he stayed at home with Marynia to look after him, while grown up excursions involved parties, theatre, nightclubs, dancing. Often Władysław and Julian set off together on their own exciting trips to the city and Julian remembered these as being some of the happiest times of all. Father and son were very close, far closer, I think, than most British fathers and young sons of the same period. My mother told me that when she took me to buy my first pair of shoes, my father insisted on coming too, taking a great interest in the fit and general stylishness of the shoes, and whether I liked them, behaviour that astonished the assistant. It was almost unheard of in the Leeds of my 1950s childhood where buying children's shoes was women's work. But it was learned behaviour on my father's part, and I'm certain my grandfather would have done exactly the same thing.

The third picture is one I find the most moving of all. Julian must be four or five years old. There are no leaves on the trees and both the ground and his little boots are covered in mud, so it's either late autumn before the snow comes, or early spring. I'd judge him to be about four and a half. His fifth birthday would be coming up in May. Gone is the baby vulnerability and the girly hairstyle and clothes. My mum and I used to call this his 'little Lord Fauntleroy' picture, after the novel by Frances Hodgson Burnett, and if you look at the cover of the old Penguin Classic edition of this book, the eponymous hero is indeed wearing a velvet suit with an elaborate collar, very similar to the one in this photograph. The classic Fauntleroy suit was a velvet cut-away jacket with matching knee pants, worn over a blouse with a large lace collar. These suits were fashionable for little boys, especially in America, but also in Britain and the rest of Europe until well into the twentieth century. It would have been quite old fashioned in Britain by the time this photograph was taken, around 1930, but it may have taken a while for the style to filter East to Poland. Or perhaps it was another manifestation of my grandfather's love for England. Nevertheless, it strikes me that the only really fancy thing about this picture is the collar and even that looks faintly out of place.

Julian is wearing a neat velvet suit with fancy buttons down the side of the short pants but everything else about him has the grimly defiant look of an active little boy who is determined to do what he wants, as soon as he possibly can. His hair is short and boyish, he has wide set dark eyes and his mouth is pursed as he scowls at the camera. I don't think he approved of the suit. It's clearly a chilly day. He is wearing a pair of extremely wrinkled woolly tights and chunky, muddy, lace-up boots and he's standing very straight with his legs planted firmly in the mud. He is holding a large billy goat firmly by the horns, as casually as though he were holding a pet dog. The goat doesn't seem too perturbed and is just waiting patiently. It's a bizarre and endearing picture, especially when you remember that the family coat of arms involved a long horned goat. Julian looks very much as you might expect Richmal Crompton's William Brown to have looked, if his mother had made him have his photograph taken wearing a velvet suit with a frilly blouse beneath. Little Lord Fauntleroy with attitude. The goat's name was Cap, pronounced Tsap. He belonged to Władysław. For some reason, he hated women. Perhaps Władysław had rescued him from somebody who had treated him cruelly. Maids, going through his pasture for milk, used to have to arm themselves with sticks, brooms and other weapons, to fend him off, because he would butt them if he got the opportunity, and those horns were hard. He loved Władysław and Julian and would run to greet them if he saw them.

On the back of this picture, somebody has written 'My beloved little Julian, a keepsake, mother.' I have only one specimen of my grandfather's handwriting, a neat and rather formal postcard written to somebody else. Many years later, long after the war, my grandmother wrote to my father, but those letters are long gone. I can't decide which of them wrote this on the back: Łucja herself, or my grandfather. The wording is unclear. My instinct is that it was written by Julian's father, because he would have been the one to take and develop the picture.

Władysław loved animals, and as well as the family dogs, he acquired or perhaps rescued, a large foreign owl called Puchacz. Puchacz lived in a specially constructed aviary, but was allowed to fly free when somebody was there to supervise him. He was very tame, so would have been bred in captivity, and would happily sit on Władek's shoulder. Dad had no idea where the owl had come from, but it may have been the enormously rare Blakiston's Fish Owl, the world's largest owl and one to be found – if it can be found at all now – in the Russian forests. A more likely alternative is the Eurasian Eagle Owl, also a very large bird, and one which is much more widely distributed.

There was a pet monkey called Fritz. Władysław, who could be jealous, in spite of his own transgressions, had maliciously named him after a German visitor who had been sweet on Łucja. Fritz was small and quick and, like Puchacz, preferred to sit on his master's shoulder when he was out and about. The family had just employed a new cook who had acquired a full set of false teeth. They were a precious item, quite difficult to procure, involving a trip to Lwów and considerable expense. She was proud of them but their possession was a matter of great shame and secrecy at that time, so she liked to pretend that they were her own beautiful white teeth. She was afraid of the monkey but, encouraged by my grandfather, finally plucked up the courage to stroke it. Startled, it leapt up and its bony little head collided with her chin. Her teeth flew across the room in a gleaming curve and she resigned on the spot, much to Łucja's dismay. My grandmother was not fond of cooking, and replacing her was going to be difficult, since good cooks were in high demand. Władysław tried to persuade her to stay, but she packed her bags and left in a state of outrage.

There are no pictures of young Julian on horseback, which is a pity, because he was placed on horseback almost as soon as he could sit upright, as befits the son of a cavalryman. At the age of eight, he was sent to buy live lobsters from the doctor in the village of Jakimów, where Karol and Wanda lived. This puzzled me at first. Lobsters are notoriously difficult to farm. But with care, it's possible to raise small numbers to maturity, which is what the doctor was doing, selling them to a select few. Little Julian rode a big, placid farm horse, with reins and a blanket, but without a saddle, the habitual way in which cavalry families taught their children to ride. He had brought a basket, one of those fishing creels with a shoulder strap, into which the doctor's housekeeper packed the lobsters. On the way back to Dziedziłow, the lid came loose and one of the lobsters escaped. Julian slid off, set the basket down and went after the escapee. He came back to find that the rest of the crustaceans had seized the opportunity of freedom, heading for the forest as best they could. He went after them and managed to retrieve them, but then realised that he was too small to remount the horse while keeping hold of the basket. It was just too high off the ground, and he had no stirrups or saddle to help him. Showing considerable ingenuity, he found a convenient ditch, so that he could park the horse there and clamber on again, hauling his basket with him. The horse seemed quite unperturbed by all these manoeuvres.

When our own son was very young, we went pony trekking here in Scotland. It was the first time Dad had ridden since he was a boy. The leader of our little party found, to her embarrassment, that her mount was badly spooked by a tractor parked in a field. It shied away every time she tried to pass.

'Excuse me,' said Dad, with his usual gentle politeness. 'But would you let me have a go? I think I can do it.'

I've never forgotten how he rode quietly ahead, past the tractor, while the spooked horse and all the rest followed on, with no further trouble. Even all those years later, he hadn't lost his touch.

In 1933, Julian went to the small school in the village, a fairly late start to formal education being the norm in most European cultures then, as it is now. There were a couple of teachers, and the children attended from eight in the morning until two in the afternoon, which gave them plenty of free time. Marynia would still come to help about the house in various ways. Sending such a young child away from home seems to have been unthinkable for his parents. The pupils at the village school were a mixed bunch, including the sons and daughters of Ruthenians and Poles living and working on the estate, those from the small farms round about, the children of the Orthodox priest, and those who might be on extended visits to the countryside for one reason or another.

All the same, Julian must have had some notion of his own status. The only story he ever told me from his time at the village school was that he had once led a strike against an overly harsh teacher, taking the rest of the pupils out in protest. It was like him that he couldn't stand bullying of any kind, and I don't think that he himself had been the teacher's victim, but one of the pupils with less standing in the small community, the kind of child who finds themselves victimised at home and then equally victimised at school. Whatever the reason, he wasn't punished for it. I suspect his father rather admired him for it.

The last picture I have of my father as a child was taken when he was about nine years old. He's much taller and more slender than the stocky little lad of previous pictures. It was again taken on the estate. It's deep winter, and he's on skis, posing for the photographer, all muffled up in a knitted hat and scarf, a warm coat and woolly trousers. As with horse-riding, skiing was essential for the sons and daughters of the *szlachta*. This is another picture in which, facially, he looks very like me, when I was about that age. There's a gate in the background, and a man wearing a big leather apron, caught in this wintry moment, in somebody else's photograph, a smith or a farrier perhaps.

When I read through the memoirs that my father wrote for me, it always strikes me that this was a country anticipating war. They might relax sufficiently to enjoy life. They might even indulge themselves in a way that seems both hedonistic and irresponsible to us, now, with our twenty-first-century Puritanism, enforced every day by social and mass media. But they must have been uncomfortably aware that it could all be destroyed in an instant. Fear of approaching chaos would have been their default setting and all plans for the future were uncertain at best. They would recognise and understand our current problems all too well. When a journalist in Ukraine, before the Russian invasion, reported that people were carrying on just as normal, and there was no panic buying, except that all the ammunition had disappeared from the shops, I thought about my grandfather and his brothers, carrying on as normal, but anticipating invasion.

One feature of this involved keeping the army up to scratch. There were few proper Army training grounds and therefore large military exercises were organised on country estates, especially those belonging to families that considered themselves to be cavalry families, which in practice meant most of them.

'In my childhood in Dziedziłow I remember at least four such occasions,' wrote Julian. 'The estate was full of soldiers and several officers were put up in one of the larger houses.'

This must have been a fascinating time for a young boy, with exercises including loading and firing big guns as well as old style cavalry charges. There were many drinking parties, inevitably, and of course these were almost always confined to men. Since the big house had one indoor toilet, and on these occasions it would be reserved exclusively for the ladies and children, the men would always go outside to pee. When one of the revellers went outside, this was the signal for perhaps five or six of them to go out together and pee companionably against a nearby garden wall. One of the cavalry officers was a little late to the party, saw several others ranged at one metre intervals against the wall and 'to create some excitement' Dad wrote, he whipped his army revolver out and began to shoot between the figures against the wall. 'On this occasion it didn't work out well because my father (i.e. Władysław) was shot in the foot. It might have been a ricochet because the injury wasn't too serious, but it certainly finished the party for that night!'

CHAPTER FOURTEEN

Seasonal Pleasures

Bogusław was unhappy about the way in which Władysław had all unexpectedly inherited Uncle Julian's property. They had been on good terms as boys, but now the baby of the family, the impetuous youngest brother, had fallen heir to large estate. Bogdan's 200 acres at Koniuch (now Khreniv) two kilometres from Dziedziłow, was not much of a consolation prize, and he wouldn't have been human if he didn't resent the good fortune of the golden child of the family. It was part of the policies of the bigger estate, but the comparison must have rankled. Even my father, as he grew a little older, noticed that resentments occasionally bubbled to the surface, some of them prompted by his aunt's family. Bogusław had married a woman my father described as 'a beautiful lady' called Niobcia, or Niobe, from a family with land near the Russian border at Czortków. Bogusław was a good, hard working farmer, while his wife was keen on the traditional female arts of cooking, preserving and distilling. Much more keen than city girl Łucja, who preferred not to go near the kitchen. Niobcia made confiture, crystallised fruits and other sweetmeats, and little Julian was always anxious to sample them, walking or riding the short distance to their house where, to give them their due, they always welcomed him. I was given confiture at various houses when I visited Poland, a double cooked fruit preserve that is difficult to make properly. Housewives would have their personal speciality cooked to their own family recipe. It was generally served on fragile porcelain dishes, to be eaten with tiny silver spoons as an accompaniment to black tea, served in tall glasses.

Bogusław, with no pretensions to be anything but the farmer he had always wanted to be, dressed informally in a fur jacket and leather boots. Years later, when Wanda showed me a heap of family photographs that she had preserved from pre-war days, all lost, alas, there was one of the two brothers, Zbigniew and Bogusław in winter, seated on a sleigh, grimly handsome young men in traditional country dress of fur-lined jackets and long leather boots, characters from a way of life that no longer exists and that fascinated me even then, back in the 1970s, so strange and foreign did it seem.

'I was a bit afraid of Uncle Bogdan,' wrote my father, 'because he had a deep voice and he was a great tease. He liked to hold onto my wrist while telling me to go away at once!' On the other hand, 'Niobcia was lovely and in fact I was a little in love with her.'

The obvious affection as well as the delicacies on offer made Julian's visits well worth while, despite the teasing. Bogusław and Niobcia had no children of their own, so they set aside any resentment against Władysław and welcomed their cheerful nephew into their house. The house that went with the land at Koniuch was small and inconvenient, so the couple decided to build themselves a new one. This was, my father remembered, a project that took a very long time and was only just completed to their satisfaction when war broke out and the couple had to flee for their lives.

The eldest brother, Zbigniew, was on much better terms with Władysław, and had no resentment at all about the good fortune of his brother's inheritance, but then he himself had the heritable tenancy of Meryszczów, arguably a better estate. He was, according to my father, 'a very nice man, but not a very good farmer'. He was unmarried and he was still suffering from the injury sustained at the battle for Lwów. With only one properly functioning lung and a serious smoking habit, he was prone to sudden bouts of ill health, especially in winter. The kind of heavy outdoor work Bogusław loved would have been quite beyond him. In spite of his physical challenges, or perhaps because of them, he used to travel to comfortable and hospitable Dziedziłow as often as possible, where he could be pampered by his young brother and his wife, neglecting his own property in the process.

'He seemed to spend far more time with us than at Meryszczów,' remarked my father.

It's clear that he was very close to his younger brother, another fact that may have begun to irritate Bogusław. The two were fanatical about chess, and taught Julian how to play, as soon as he was old enough to grasp the rules. Especially in winter, they used to play well into the small hours. Occasionally the games would extend from eleven o'clock in the morning until two o'clock the following morning, with breaks for sandwiches and drinks whenever they began to feel hungry. Who knows what long-suffering Łucja thought about it all, but they used to invent their own rules, such as starting with two pawns at once. Julian remembered this causing him some embarrassment when, as he grew older, he assumed that this was the way chess was always played, and tried to do it in other company.

Shooting was an autumn or winter pursuit. Władysław used to hold shoots for a select few guests, often friends from the city, with beaters and some six to eight guns. The game consisted of foxes, which were seen as pests, hares, pheasant and grouse. The hunts were to cull and curb the wild populations and there were rules that were strictly observed: no shooting out of season and no shooting of sitting creatures. They were an all day affair, with hot food transported to the woods on long carts, in earthenware dishes packed into straw. This would almost always involve the traditional bigos, or hunters' stew, a slow cooked mix of meat and vegetables, including sauerkraut, often served with bread. Cooks and housewives would have their own particular recipes for bigos and there was a certain amount of competition involved. I ate so much bigos over a Christmas visit to Warsaw in the 1970s – it was served in every house as a matter of course – that I wished never to see it again, but it is delicious, and must have been a very welcome lunch in the middle of a chilly autumn day. Hares in particular, of which there were many, would be a good addition to the family table. Unlike now, when skips full of dead pheasants shot for 'sport' are fairly commonplace, other than foxes, you always ate what you killed. There was no waste.

When I read about those few years, from my father's memoir, I find a patchwork of impressions of the turning seasons, but most of all I get the sense of a close community. There were extremes of poverty and privilege, it's true. There was a busy social life revolving around the house at

Dziedziłow with a comfortable web of familial and friendship connections. They may not always have been cordial, but they were loving. Wanda and Karol, Bogusław and Niobcia and the Hanakowskis were all close by. Danuta divided her time between her father's house at Feliksa and her stepbrother's house at Dziedziłow. Zbigniew was almost a fixture, but there would have been frequent visits from other family and friends, including Ludmiła and Feliks, bringing a whiff of Warsaw glamour with them, as well as Łucja's quiet unmarried sister from Lwów, and the large and unconventional Kossak family, telling tales of a Bohemian world far beyond the predictable life of the village.

Did my grandmother enjoy these parties? Or did she sometimes grow weary of a house full of people and a husband with a roving eye? It was what she had signed up for when she married him, but had she understood the reality of it? She was a city girl born and bred, and I wonder if she grew tired of the mud in spring and autumn, the snow and ice in winter, and the invasions of flies and yet more visitors during the hot summer months. Did the relative dearth of modern conveniences irritate her: the uncertain electricity and water supply? There were nightingales singing in the gardens, amusing parties, holidays and enough visits to Lwów and elsewhere to keep her happy. Władysław's car was a bonus and meant that they could drive to her beloved city throughout spring and summer. But did she have her doubts about it all? I'm sure she did. Władysław worked hard, if not always efficiently. Even many years later, people who had known him and liked him, people who had benefited from his generosity, were quick to remind me of his kindness and his enthusiasm. If he worked hard, he played very hard indeed. In the light of what was to come, I'm glad he made the most of his time. But I find myself thinking of my grandmother with some sympathy. Perhaps life was not quite the fairy-tale that she had anticipated, and things were about to get a good deal worse.

One intriguing story helps to illustrate the near constant stream of visitors, and some of the possible reasons for their presence at Dziedziłow. In the village cemetery there is a Czerkawski family tomb, in which is buried Dr Julian, who gave Władysław his inheritance, and my great grandmother Anna, with her dates from 1871 to 1925 and the surnames from her two marriages: Czerkawska and Hanakowska. These inscriptions are pictured online, with photographs of the tombstone itself. On that same cemetery site is a picture of the whole tombstone, and right down at the bottom, you can see another name: Zulenka Poklewska Koziełł. The inscription reads 'of our village, born in 1925 and died in 1932.'

The Poklewska Koziełł family were Poles with business interests in pre-revolutionary Russia. They seem to have made a fortune as industrialists, all of which they lost during the Revolution, although at least one of their impressive palaces survives in Belarus and has undergone renovation. Zulenka is possibly a pet name. Zoia de Stoeckl was the wife of Alfons Poklewski Koziełł who was born in Russia in 1891. This would make him roughly the right age to be Zulenka's father, which makes me wonder if Zulenka was named Zoia for her mother. Some of the family tree is privately held so it's hard to confirm any of this.

Sadly, she died while still a child of six or seven, but the inscription 'of our village' suggests that she was born in Dziedziłow or possibly came there in infancy. Her birth year was the year before my father's, but he didn't remember her or at least he never spoke of her. Maybe she was simply one of the various children he played with. I haven't been able to find out anything else about her, but we do know that Alfons died in England in 1962.

The most likely explanation for her short life in Dziedziłow is that her parents, fleeing the Soviets, had somehow washed up there, and were living in one of the estate houses for a while before moving west for their own safety. Given the events of the next few years, it's as well they maintained a certain secrecy about their background and escaped to the UK. Nevertheless, the very fact that little Zulenka was buried in the Czerkawski family tomb, along with Julian and Anna, the fact that somebody – in all likelihood my grandfather – paid for a loving inscription for her, suggests that she was of great importance in their lives, although the rest remains yet another tantalising mystery.

As well as social occasions, the Dziedziłow year was marked by various religious and traditional folk festivals, existing side by side and equally well observed. One of the pagan early spring festivals involved the Marzanna, the Slavic goddess associated with winter and death but also natural wisdom, rebirth and dreams, who perhaps finds her equivalent in the Celtic Cailleach, the wise hag, who must go to sleep before springtime can come again. On the first day of spring, in March, people made a straw effigy of this goddess, dressed her in white and decorated her with coloured ribbons. Then, she was burned and drowned in running water. The spectators must avoid touching her, and as they left, must not look back at her at all, nor must they slip and fall down. This is a folk custom that survives to this day in parts of the Slavic world.

As the local landowner, Władysław was on good terms with the Orthodox priest who was frequently invited for meals. Easter was a traditional and religious celebration in both churches. Eggs were blown or hard boiled and decorated with various dyes, or pieces of fabric, or hand painted. People took carefully prepared baskets of food, always including hard boiled eggs, to the church to be blessed. They grew little trays of grass, to accommodate white sugar lambs, in honour of the 'lamb of God.' One of the Easter cakes was *przekładaniec*, a huge, achingly sweet cake with chocolate, cream and sometimes dates, marzipan and plum jam, built up in layers. Less sweet, but equally rich, was the moulded cream cheese *pascha wielkanocna*, often made in a clay flowerpot, turned out and decorated. The house was decorated too with flowers and greenery and the Lenten fast was broken in style with an enormous meal of eggs, ham, cheese, pickles and all kinds of baked goods, including sweet yeast cakes made with a dozen eggs at a time, and luscious baked cheesecakes.

In summer, there were family holidays as well as more frequent trips to Lwów, although Władysław and Łucja rarely went abroad. There would be excursions to the seaside, to Gdynia on the Baltic Coast, to the Mazurian Lakes, the Beskid Mountains and Truskawiec, south of Lwów, a fashionable spa town, with health giving water that had a strong taste of diesel, not surprisingly since the Polish oil fields were only sixty kilometres away. This place was destined to become significant for the family in more ways than one.

In autumn they would have to deal with an abundant fruit harvest which was either sent to the city to be sold, or preserved in various ways for the household to use throughout the coming winter. In winter the family would go on skiing holidays, travelling to Zakopane and Krynica in the Tatra mountains, by a train known as the 'ski-bridge'. This journey involved travelling twenty kilometres by horse drawn sleigh to Zadwórze, followed by fifty kilometres by train to Lwów and then an overnight train journey via Kraków to Zakopane. Holidays like this were not for the faint hearted, but the adults would relieve the monotony by eating and drinking and playing bridge on the way.

Winters in the Lwów region were harsh, since that part of Poland was very far from either the Baltic or the Black Sea. The various estates and the villages surrounding them became isolated by the weather. The only vehicular traffic in winter consisted of horse drawn sleighs and even these were limited to the flat and eminently practical country sleigh, often used for transporting produce. These had wide runners which did not sink in deep snow. The driver sat on a bale of straw and passengers travelled in a prone position on a platform of wood and straw, covered with a large sheepskin rug. This was very comfortable, said my father, although remembering that poor Anna had given birth to Władysław on one of these contraptions, I can't say I envy her.

The snow usually started a little before Christmas which had its own traditions and customs. The main Christmas celebration was, as it remains in most Catholic countries, on Christmas Eve, although on 6th December, St Nicholas's Eve, St Nicholas himself, dressed in red and white, came into the house, hauling a sack full of presents for the local children behind him. Julian noticed that St Nicholas always kissed Łucja's hand very attentively, although it was a few years before he realised that it was his father. Sometimes this character was accompanied by a very realistic devil with a tail and horns. His job was to pretend that the children had been naughty and not nearly nice enough, although the gifts were always forthcoming in the end.

The Orthodox Priest, his wife and four children usually came to the Christmas Eve supper. Any close family living nearby and people who had no children were invited, so the numbers varied, but an extra place was always set for the uninvited visitor who might be Christ himself and had to be welcomed accordingly. This was a sumptuous but meatless meal. There were twelve dishes, including *barszcz*, the traditional beetroot soup with a swirl of sour cream on top, fish of various sorts, always including carp, sometimes set in jelly, delicious but bony. There was pierogi with potato and cheese or mushroom and cabbage fillings. In Dziedziłow and Meryszczów, the dessert was a dish called *kutia*, a traditional rich porridge, made with cooked, ground poppyseeds, cream, honey, dried fruit and also, in this part of Poland, cooked grains of wheat. Władysław liked to supervise the making of this dessert, calling for more cream to make it palatable. Like many of these traditional winter puddings or frumenties, of which our own Christmas pudding is only one example, they tend to be an acquired taste. I certainly like it, but not everyone does. Best of all, is the Christmas cake called *makowiec*, a rich yeast pastry encasing a luscious filling of ground poppyseed and fruit.

Pieces of straw were placed under the linen cloth. This was a method of divination in which each guest pulled out a piece and looked at the length and quality of the stalk. The longer and stronger the better. Mindful of the religious nature of the feast, guests also exchanged small pieces of white wafer called *opłatek*. Blessed by the priest, this would bring good fortune for the year ahead. Towards the end of the meal, a bell rang, which meant that the angel was coming. The Christmas tree always shook at this moment, which greatly impressed Julian at the time. There were gifts under the tree, mostly for the children, but a few for the host and hostess. There was always a real tree, lit by candles, and decorated with glass baubles, sugar birdcages, sugar mice and gingerbread men. Till the day he died my father wouldn't countenance an artificial tree and we always had a real one, the selection of which was a significant event in the pre-Christmas period. I've followed in his footsteps and can't bear artificial trees. On Christmas Day, there were visits to nearby family and friends if they could be managed through the snow. There would be a good meal in the middle of the day which passed very much as Christmas Day here, with the difference that large quantities of bigos were served instead of turkey.

The period of mid January and the whole of February, called Luty, the severe one, was particularly challenging. There were few additional snowfalls, but there was always a sustained frost, and the temperature could fall as low as 20 degrees celsius. The harvest was in, the preserving all done, including flavoured vodkas to keep out the cold, and ice was stored in the ice house for the coming summer. Wood for the winter had already been chopped and stored, with last year's mature timber used first, and the cattle were indoors. The livestock had to be cared for, and properties maintained, but there was little else to be done. Most people battened down the hatches, waited for spring and hoped that their supplies would hold out. There was local skiing, as well as trips further afield, pond skating and 'ski-ring', a sport in which five or six people on skis were towed along behind a horse, with one of them holding the reins, while the rest held precariously onto ropes and sticks.

For those with more means at their disposal, however, this was the time of the *Kulig*, literally meaning 'sleigh ride'. A family asked the groom to get their biggest sleigh ready and set off for a neighbouring estate, usually starting in the early evening. These were horse drawn sleighs with bells attached to the horse collars, so that you always heard them coming in spite of the silence of the snow. Not that the party itself was silent in any way. Far from it. Women and occasionally children participated as well as men. They arrived with a lot of shouting and singing. '*Jednemy z Kuligiem* – we are travelling with the *Kulig*!' (Literally 'at one with the Kulig!') The potential host could not possibly ignore this arrival, even if the family were in bed at the time. Much like the old first footers in Scotland, a custom more honoured in remembrance than in reality now in most places, the *Kulig* party had to be entertained. There was food, a lot of drinking and dancing and then both families, each using their own transport, went to the next estate and so on, gathering a cavalcade of sleighs and people along the way, like a giant snowball.

My father described one memorable January when eight horse drawn sleighs full of people arrived at 3am. They practically ate the larder empty and drank the cellar dry, after which Władysław and Łucja got out their own sleigh and led them to the home of the Orthodox priest, about three miles away, almost ruining him in the process. These *Kuligs* went on for days, with some of the earlier participants quietly retiring from exhaustion. *Kuligs* were usually deemed to be much too wild for children, but if they were going to a near neighbour, Julian went along too, and was sent back with a servant or his nanny before the party became too rowdy.

'To me the journeys were the most exciting thing about them,' wrote my father. 'I can still hear the swishing of sleighs on snow and the jingling of bells and harness, while I was all snug and warm cuddled up on sheepskin, on a brilliant, frosty night.'

Zhivago again.

Julian must have been about this age, when he experienced one of the strangest 'told as true' stories I've ever heard – and I'm fond of the occasional ghost story. This one strays into chilling M R James territory, inexplicable and full of foreboding. One bright, moonlit night in autumn, he was driving home from the station at Zadwórze with his father. They had come back from Lwów by train, unexpectedly, and very late in the evening. He couldn't remember the purpose of the journey, nor why they had come back earlier than anticipated. He and his father often took excursions to Lwów for various reasons connected with the estate. Usually transport would be sent for them, but on this occasion, they had had to beg a lift, and they were being driven by a farmhand in an ordinary farmer's cart, with sheaves of straw to sit on.

It was the time of year when manure had been put on the fields. The farm workers would empty half a cart into a big pile to be left for the frosts to do their work, so that it could be spread out later when the weather grew warmer. The large field had several large piles. As they passed by, at a leisurely trot, they spied a figure standing up on one of the heaps, which was odd in itself, since it was a mild night, the substance was very soft and the figure should have sunk in, but it didn't. The moonlight, said Dad, cast odd shadows and it was impossible to tell the precise shape. It was the size of a child, but it didn't have the look of a child. Not at all. It was small and wiry and uncanny. Always curious, Władysław asked the driver to draw the horse to a halt.

As they watched, the creature suddenly bent right over backwards, like a spring in motion, an impossible contortion, and as it did so, it cried out loudly, 'he hee!' Then, smoothly, it coiled forwards, to the extreme of the bow shape, and cried 'ha haa!' It was, said Dad later, both comical and sinister. Not surprisingly, the driver crossed himself and tried to leave, but Władysław said 'wait!' He wanted a better look.

The creature leapt onto another pile of manure and repeated the contortion.

'He hee! Ha haa!'

In the cart, impulsive Władysław got to his feet, cupped his hands and shouted back, 'He hee, ha haa!' bending over as he did so, mocking it. Julian tugged at his father's coat in alarm. But the creature had heard. It turned in their direction, and then it was moving towards them with extreme and horrible rapidity. Władysław grabbed the whip from the petrified driver, and whipped up the horse. They arrived home in record time, all three of them sweating with fear and laughing hysterically.

When I told this story later on, wondering what it could possibly be, friends remarked on its similarity to a bogle, a repulsive creature that would lurk in the fields, waiting to scare the life out of unwary travellers. Robert Burns has his Tam o' Shanter 'glow'rin round wi' prudent cares lest bogles catch him unawares.' The Slav equivalent is the *polevik*. These are dangerous field spirits, deformed creatures with grass instead of hair who also lie in wait for unwary travellers. The daylight version always seems more terrifying to me: the noon ghost, the beautiful woman in white who enchants you on a summer's day, but who will cut off your head with her shears if you offend her.

CHAPTER FIFTEEN

The Affair

In 1934, a longed-for daughter named Teresa was born to Wanda and Karol, a cousin for Julian. Not long after, the family sold Jakimów and moved to a villa in Tatarów on the River Prut in the Carpathians where Karol produced a series of paintings of the *Hucul* mountain people in their traditional dress. These were a specific ethnic group of mountain men and women from Western Ukraine and Romania, many of them shepherds, leading a nomadic life. Theirs is an ancient culture of colourful and intricate crafts, including clothing, sculpture, architecture, wood and metalwork. They play traditional musical instruments such as the bagpipes and the *tsymbaly* and they sing mountain songs with that powerful vibrato that carries long distances, from hillside to hillside. All of this proved inspirational for Karol among many other artists and writers, and his pictures of these people sold well, but I wonder if Wanda was happy to leave her familiar surroundings and the family she had been close to for so long? Well, maybe she enjoyed the change, being an enterprising young woman, and besides, there were rumblings of unrest at Dziedziłow, the small intimations of an earthquake that would soon disturb the whole family.

Wanda in particular was already feeling unsettled after the birth. Then, one of their windows was broken when somebody threw a stone at their house. Although this may have been a village child or a mischievous adolescent rather than a serious attack, it seems to have crystallised their desire to move. Even though his Hucul paintings would become successful, Karol still wasn't making much money. They bought a plot of land in Tatarów and built a house for themselves, a two storey wooden chalet, like so many buildings in this area. The project had used up all their small capital and more. Wanda, wondering how she could contribute, decided that they would open a guest house or 'pension' to use the continental expression at the time. Like the guest houses in Truskawiec, it was called a villa, in this case Villa Teresa, after their little daughter. 'They' however meant Wanda and whatever help they could afford to employ. Karol was single-mindedly devoted to his painting, and that was never going to change. Wanda wasn't the best cook in the world at that time, but they employed a cook to cater for the visitors, and Wanda herself undertook everything else, including all kinds of projects aimed at making the place a success. She already had some knowledge of beekeeping from her years at Meryszczów and Jakimów. She did the housework, grew vegetables, set up an apiary and even raised a pig to provide meat for the table.

At first, the Villa Teresa was a great success, partly I think, because Karol himself was an attraction for the various artists who came to Tatarów to be inspired, much as artists would flock to Cornwall and Kirkcudbright for similar inspiration. How much more inspiring then, to stay in the same house as the famous Juliusz Kossak's grandson, or

Wojciech Kossak's nephew? They were not short of artist and intellectual visitors. Karol was flattered by this attention. As a young woman, Wanda had made many friends from other *szlachta* families, and they too came to stay. These included Władysław, Łucja and little Julian, but the Villa Teresa also attracted the rich and famous. Pianist Artur Rubinstein was one of them, widely regarded even now as one of the greatest pianists of all time. In 1932, aged 45, he had married Nela Młynarska, a 24-year-old Polish ballerina. At Villa Teresa, where Karol had a piano and played with more enthusiasm than skill, his friends jokingly encouraged him to play in front of the master.

'Of course I will,' he said. 'But only if Artur will draw a horse first!'

Karol was often moody and sometimes given to fits of depression, especially in the winter months. He missed his brother-in-law and would sometimes head off to Lwów or Kraków, leaving Wanda and Teresa to cope with the guest house in Tatarów without him. Perhaps they got on better without his attractive but volatile presence. The marriage at that stage can't have been entirely idyllic, but there's no doubt that Wanda loved him and made the best of things. There were few alternatives and by the time I met them, they were clearly as close as two people can be who have literally been through the wars together.

It was in this same unsettling year that Zbigniew Czerkawski became very ill. He was still a heavy smoker which didn't help. Now he developed tuberculosis in his remaining lung. Somehow, the family managed to get the money together to send him to a sanatorium in Dubrovnik.

Writing about it in retrospect, my father pointed out that this must have cost a fortune, and wondered how they could possibly have afforded it, given that the estate at Meryszczów wasn't thriving. I think Władysław, always more generous than practical, had helped him out as best he could, and perhaps Łucja was less than happy about the amount of money involved.

Sadly, it was all in vain. Not long after he came back, he died, whereupon the family discovered that he had willed his estate to Władysław, who now had both Meryszczów and Dziedziłow in his care. Władysław must have known about his brother's intentions, but I suspect he had kept quiet about them. Unsurprisingly, this created even more ill feeling between Władysław and Bogusław. Niobcia's family in particular felt that they had been shabbily treated and didn't hesitate to make those feelings clear. The couple found it hard to conceal their resentment, although the run-down estate at Meryszczów was something of a poison chalice. With the right owner at the helm, it certainly had potential, but was my grandfather that owner?

Juliah wrote that 'the plan was to sell off Dziedziłow, and enlarge or overhaul Meryszczów, but I don't think it was very successful, inasmuch as Dziedziłow was gradually reduced, while Meryszczów didn't seem to thrive at all.'

It's hard not to imagine that Bogusław would have made a better job of reviving the fortunes of the estate. Moreover, Władysław had other more personal matters on his mind, and was about to incur significant expenses because of them.

1934 seems to have been a tipping point for the family. As ever, knowing dates gives some clue as to the reasons why things happen. I think my grandfather missed the company of his chess-playing elder brother and his artist brother-in-law. Not only that, but his inheritance of another estate meant that (like his stepfather before him) he would have to travel there, at least to see what needed to be done. All the same, I suspect the seeds of change may have been sown a little earlier, perhaps on one of those family holidays in Truskawiec, where the spa waters tasted of oil, holidays that my father remembered with nothing but pleasure. There are plenty of existing photographs and postcards of that era. It's not hard to see that this was a glamorous resort in the late 1920s and 30s, one in which Hercule Poirot would not have been out of place, solving crimes of passion and intrigue. There are gardens, pavilions, gazebos and large hotels in plenty, although they are called 'villas' and have names such as Villa Olga, or Villa Beautiful or Villa Marja Helena. Central to the resort is the ultra fashionable Club Towarzyski, the 'social club'. This has a long, low spa house, with an adjoining club and restaurant, all gleaming with white paint. Outside, trees are cut into fancy topiary shapes, so that they shade numerous tables, with a few umbrellas and palm trees thrown in for good measure. There are comfortable basket chairs in which fashionable people, dressed in their best outfits, congregate, taking the waters, and other more palatable drinks. They are smoking, reading newspapers, chatting and generally enjoying themselves, seeing and being seen, amid an ambiance of privilege and style. And flirting. There was plenty of flirting.

I think it was here, while he was on holiday with Łucja and Julian, that Władysław first met an exceptionally pretty and fashionable woman called Rozalia Maciuk, née Hladka. She was the wife of a schoolteacher called Jaroslav Maciuk, or Matsiuk in the Ukrainian spelling, and it's possible that she herself came from Truskawiec. Certainly, she and Jaroslav had a son named Orest in 1932. This is confirmed by his later obituaries, because he became a notable historian in Ukraine, a man who died suddenly and sadly of a heart attack in 1999, four years after my father. I have photocopies of a few tiny snapshots of some of the Maciuk family members that Orest's daughter sent to me back in 2002, and young Orest is the very image of Jaroslav, although one of these pictures wrongly labels Jaroslav himself as a Czerkawski. I would like to have met Orest, or at least corresponded with him, but it was not to be.

Writing about these events many years later, Julian speculated that his father's affair with Rozalia began in 1934 or '35, not long after Zbigniew's death and the Kossak family departure. He also wrote that it progressed while they were at Dziedziłow, that she and her husband were living some eight miles away, and that Władysław would 'ride over to spend time with her while her schoolteacher husband was at work'. There are a few problems with this. Julian would have been about eight years old at the time, and although we can have clear memories of challenging situations at that age, we sometimes conflate the details. I can find no evidence that Rozalia's husband ever lived and worked eight miles from Dziedziłow. There is, however, some evidence of a connection with Przemyślany, which is six or seven kilometres from the family estate at Meryszczów and a very easy distance on horseback for a determined young man with a good excuse for visiting his second estate.

In 1991, an elderly lady wrote to me, offering some information about the couple, saying that she had been friendly with Rozalia and my grandfather and that she too had lived in Przemyślany and had been married to a schoolteacher herself. I think it's safe to assume that Władysław had begun to travel between his two estates, much as Anna and Jan Hanakowski had done when the Czerkawski children were young. I think while he was at Meryszczów, he renewed an acquaintance with the attractive married woman he had already met while they were on holiday in Truskawiec.

This relationship was serious, more serious than any of his other flirtations.

Julian, gradually becoming aware of the rift between his parents, must have been torn. He was in many ways closer to his father than he was to his mother, and yet like all children placed in that situation, he hated it, felt betrayed. His father had strayed before, no doubt about it. But Łucja had been content to turn a blind eye, so long as she perceived these relationships to be dalliances. This was clearly more serious and more threatening to her own position, her stability. He remembered the sense of impending doom. Knew that Rozalia was 'a very strong character' and probably a little older than Łucja and a few years older than Władysław as well. My chief emotion when I saw pictures of her was one of surprise. I think this may have been because I had firmly fixed in my mind the notion that my grandmother was the flighty one, that the couple had married young (which was true, even for those days) and that my grandfather had found a more intelligent woman willing to share his life. Intelligent she may well have been, but Rozalia was also an exceptionally attractive woman wearing ultra fashionable clothes. In one of the snapshots, she's swathed in an expensive fur collar, the kind with the legs and sometimes the head of the original owner of the pelt still attached. In another, she's perched on a bridge, holding her clutch bag, wearing a fancy hat and smart costume. She is, it has to be said, very lovely.

'My mother called her a great many unflattering names within my hearing,' wrote my father. This was something she had never done before, or not in his presence. He had never been so aware of the growing split between his parents, and it alarmed him. His mother's intense and understandable dislike of Mrs Maciuk certainly influenced him. The family soldiered on, struggling to maintain stability for another couple of years, with Władysław spending time at Meryszczów, sometimes with his wife and son, sometimes by himself. It's clear that he also took any opportunity to spend time with his mistress in nearby Przemyślany. What did Jaroslav and her son Orest think of all this? Did Orest know what was going on? He was so young that it would have been easy enough to shield him from it. An interesting letter from one of Orest's own children, born quite late in his life, remarks that he married at the age of twenty-two, while pursuing a distinguished academic career, divorced and remarried, very happily, but had almost no contact with his mother until many years later, just before she died in Warsaw.

Worse than all of this, from my father's point of view, the letter from Rozalia's friend implied that Władysław and Łucja were divorced, and somewhere online I found an inaccurate family tree propagating this information.

'My parents were never divorced!' wrote my father, with uncharacteristic indignation. I spoke to him about this, but I have seldom seen him so furious. Not with me, although I found myself wishing I had never raised it with him at all. He was deeply uncomfortable with his memories of an untenable situation and one that, because of subsequent events, he had never been able to remedy or resolve. Łucja and Władysław never were divorced, partly because it so seldom happened in their circles, unless cruelty was involved, and even then not often. Who knows what would have happened in the future, but occupation and war would very soon make all other considerations superfluous.

'My parents were separated in 1936. My mother and I moved into a flat in Lwów, with her sister Nusia and that was where I went to school,' wrote my father. 'But they were never divorced.'

They had moved to a four-bedroom flat on Ulica Listopada, a lovely part of the city, although it must have been an expensive part of the city too. There were other considerations. My grandfather wanted to sell off a large proportion of Dziedziłow, leaving a more compact estate, one that could be run by a competent manager. He was planning to invest the capital thus realised in Meryszczów, which Zbigniew had neglected. Beyond that, there was the question of Julian's education. The village school wasn't providing him with much stimulation, but his parents were still reluctant to send him to boarding school until he was older. The couple agreed on this, if on little else, that he would be better served by a school in Lwów, followed by boarding school later on, if he seemed that way inclined. Changing times meant that a day school in the city was more likely, even if war hadn't intervened. The possibility of him training as an artist was still on the table. Łucja had never really taken to country living, so perhaps she was happier in Lwów, even though her son wasn't.

The reality was that, like many impulsive young men, Władysław had placed himself in the unenviable position of running three homes at once: the flat in Lwów, the estate at Dziedziłów and another one at Meryszczów. He was spending a certain amount of money on Mrs Maciuk as well, given that her husband may have been even less happy with his wife's behaviour than Łucja. Rozalia's old friend, who seems to have had something of a crush on him, describes Władysław as a 'charming man'. Throughout, confusingly, she calls her friend 'Nusia', which may have been a middle name, since all Orest's obituaries call his mother Rozalia. She points out that Zbigniew had left the estate in a bad way, and that it was only owing to Władysław that it 'was restored'. The second half of this statement is manifestly untrue, for reasons which will become clear. She tells me that Rozalia and Władysław lived at Meryszczów. But my father writes that he 'spent some long holidays with my father after the separation. Mrs Maciuk was never there.'

These must have been bewildering and unhappy years for Julian. Occasionally his father visited him and Łucja in Lwów, but the atmosphere was always strained. Julian visited Dziedziłow and Meryszczów, only ever with his father, and confessed that he was happier there. They visited Uncle Karol and Aunt Wanda in Tatarów, and once or twice Julian stayed with Bogusław and his wife, who maintained their fondness for their nephew.

Rozalia's friend then tells me, somewhat tactlessly, given whose daughter and grand-daughter I am, that her friend 'had her own son, and to tell you the truth, Władysław was stand-offish and cold towards him. He told her that he loved only *his* own son, and she would just have to reconcile herself to it.'

As long as there was some small suspicion that Orest could have been Władysław's son, I had some sympathy for Rozalia. I think my father, who had been too young to understand the details, harboured the same suspicions. But Władysław was not in the habit of denying his own children. Quite the opposite. Now, with the near certainty that Orest was, in fact, Jaroslav's son, born long before the affair began, a lovely, bright boy who looked exactly like his father, who would go on to become distinguished in his own field, and whose early death would sadden many, I can also understand Władysław, harsh as his words may seem. He may have been a philanderer and an adulterer, but he was also *szlachta*, and he was making it clear that his inheritance, with all the traditional rights and responsibilities that went with it, were wholly focused on Julian. For him, whether you agree with him or not, whether you approve or not, there would have been no other possibility whatsoever. I wish I could have talked about this to my father, but I couldn't. I think it was much too painful. For some time,

I wished I had never started researching these relationships at all, wished I had let all those sleeping dogs rest in peace. But now that the protagonists are themselves all at peace, with both boys having made the very best of their lives, I think that there is a sense in which both Orest and Julian were victims. Orest must have been bitterly disappointed in his mother and Julian couldn't help being disappointed in his father, while still loving him with all his heart – a very grown-up morass of emotions to be experienced by children who were still far from mature themselves.

Finally, Rozalia's friend also sends me a photocopy of a postcard from the spa club at Truskawiec. She received it from my grandfather in January of 1939, an odd time to be in a spa town and an oddly cold message from one who was supposed to be a close friend. It sends greetings from Truskawiec and is signed in the most formal and autocratic way possible, with the surname only. Pulling rank. Poles, like their language, are good at formality. By that time, the political situation was deteriorating rapidly, and Władysław had begun to see the necessity of taking precautions in case the worst happened. I'm not sure that even he could have predicted what that worst might be and just how bad things would become.

CHAPTER SIXTEEN

Russian Occupation

When I was researching and writing this book, I did some of it to the accompaniment of the alluring Polish tango music that was so much a feature of the interwar years. It was an appropriate soundtrack, more appropriate perhaps than Zhivago. When, in 1918, Poland had re-established its full independence after 120 years of conflict, the joyous feeling of hope for a new future in the new decade, coupled with the caution borne of long experience, spawned, among other things, a thriving musical and satirical theatre culture. We mostly associate this with pre-war Germany, and the film based on Isherwood's Berlin stories, but there was a thriving and edgy cabaret scene in Poland too, arguably even more prominent and popular than among the country's German neighbours. These were the years of the *Kabaret Literacki,* or literary cabaret, involving comedy, monologues, and satirical songs. Although Warsaw was the centre of this fashion, Lwów, with a long tradition of theatre and a thriving café culture was not far behind, with revue theatres and cabarets such as Ul and Chochlik and a radio show called 'Wesoła Lwówska Fala' which roughly translates as the 'Happy Lwów Wave'.

The Jazz Age was not just a feature of the USA, and in an illuminating essay on the subject, Juliette Bretan points out the beauty and complexity of songs and performances from the 1920s and '30s, encouraged by a growing sense of Polish internationalism and multiculturalism. The burgeoning film industry in Warsaw also contributed, with some four thousand tangos composed during this period. All too soon, though, we have the sad, doom laden *Złociste Chryzantemy*, Golden Chrysanthemums, by Janusz *Popławski* (not to be confused with a modern and much more scurrilous version). This is a cry from the heart of a cheated lover. 'Golden chrysanthemums in a crystal vase. I reach out to them and whisper, why have you left me?' This was perhaps the last tango recorded in Warsaw before the outbreak of WW2. Perceptively, Bretan calls it an 'expression of desperate nostalgia for something forever lost'. In the case of this song, a woman laments her lost lover. Soon almost everything would be lost. As so many of the Jewish musicians, writers and singers were murdered in concentration camps and ghettoes, their Polish counterparts and companions were destined for the Soviet Gulags. Meanwhile, the Nazis destroyed even the record factories, smashing any remaining records into tiny pieces.

In 1939, Germany and Russia, then in cahoots, seemed set to carve up Poland between them, with Russia threatening yet again to occupy Lwów and significant parts of Galicia. In these circumstances, Władysław's initial plan, as daring and impractical as so many of his plans, was to head south and try to get across the border to Hungary or Romania, both of which routes were feasible during the summer of 1939. It may have seemed unworkable, but many people

managed to do just that, and had he not overcompli-
cated his life already, had he not been determined to save
Dziedziłow and Meryszczów and those who depended on
the estates for their livelihoods, he might have joined his
little family in Lwów sooner and taken them to ultimate
safety. He hesitated and was lost. Nevertheless, much of his
concern at this time seems to have been for his son. He and
Łucja settled their differences sufficiently to make plans
and, as I've previously described, send him south with
his Uncle Bogusław and Aunt Niobcia, to try to cross into
Romania before the inevitable border closure. Did he have
some of his mind on Rozalia? Of course he did. His priority was Julian, but he would certainly have been worrying
about her as well. And wanting to spend time with her.

While Julian was travelling south with his uncle and
aunt, Władysław was delayed at Dziedziłow, trying to make
arrangements for the safety of the workers there, should
the Russians arrive in force. The splits in the community
between Ukrainians, some but not all of them Bolsheviks,
and Poles, as well as a significant Jewish population would
not have made things any easier, but Władysław had a
conscience where his estate was concerned, if not always
about the women in his life. Was he conflicted about all
this? Was he agonising about protecting the mother of
his child and leaving his mistress behind in Przemyślany?
I'm sure he was. He would have worried about his sister,
Ludmiła, in Warsaw with her soldier husband. His young
step-sister Danuta had already moved away and was working as a nurse by this time, possibly also in Warsaw. As with
so many of his friends and relations, her nephew Julian

completely lost touch with her and throughout his life assumed that she had died in the war, an assumption that turned out to be false.

Meanwhile, Władysław, with no immediate means of knowing, could only assume that his brother and son had managed to escape to Hungary. He wondered if Łucja might have gone too. They still weren't on good terms, but all he could think about at this time was his son. His best course of action was to try to get to Hungary himself in the hope of meeting his family there. It is perhaps even more difficult for us now to understand the immense danger, the threat to life, of being outed as a member of the *szlachta*, or landowning classes, or an intellectual, or somebody with military connections, under Soviet rule. It was, in effect, a death sentence. You could try to hide, or you could flee. These were your only choices.

Upon his arrival in Hungary, which was now a member of the axis powers, no friend to Russia, but no friend to Poland either, Władysław was promptly interned by the authorities there. The internment must have been more half-hearted than would have been expected under Russian rule, because he soon escaped and managed to slip back over the border to Truskawiec, where he met Rozalia. Back in Poland, he got word that Julian had been unable to cross the border and had come home all by himself, but that his son and wife were now relatively safe in Lwów. For the moment, there was little else to be done except to keep his head down and try to avoid the occupying Russian authorities, whose detestation of Polish landowners with military training knew no bounds and who intended to deal with them as quickly as possible, preferably by tying their hands behind their backs and shooting them in the head. Truskawiec was big enough for him to be able to maintain a low profile. He daren't go back to either of his estates. And travelling to Lwów was fraught with danger, not least because he feared that somebody might betray him as *szlachta* in the city and thus betray his wife and son as well.

Uncle Bogusław and Aunt Niobcia, despairing of any escape over the southern border, eventually moved back to Lwów and stayed with Łucja and Julian for a while. Then, casting about for possible solutions to their dangerous *szlachta* origins, and denunciation as counter-revolutionaries, they thought it might be easier to maintain a low profile in the part of Poland that had been occupied by the Germans. Bogusław looked what he was, a small farmer, and that was what they would say his occupation was. They thought that he would surely be able to find work. While they were waiting and planning, Bogusław worked as a dustman for a while. He had worked hard on his own small acreage for years, was a fit man, still in his thirties, and physical labour was the best possible disguise.

In 1940, he and his wife managed to get across what was known as the 'green border' to German occupied Poland and Bogusław secured a position as manager of a small estate there. If he had been able to keep his head down and work, all might yet have been well, but these were precarious times. Overall, during the German occupation of pre-war Polish territory, the Nazis murdered three million Jews and two and a half million Poles. There was no puppet government in Poland, unlike in some other parts of Europe, and there were limited numbers of collaborators. There was the Home Army, whose *raison d'etre* was resistance, come what may, and whose record where collaboration was concerned was clean, but there were other groups of so called 'partisans' some of whom might loathe the Nazis but were no fans of the Poles either. Some were right wing and anti-communist, some were left wing, some were nationalist. The communist underground denounced Home Army operatives to the Nazis. It was, in short, a mess of gigantic proportions, with various groups vying for supremacy in deadly fashion. A group of armed men came to the small estate that Bogusław was managing, trying to requisition grain and animals. It was not in him to be subservient, however dangerous the situation. He objected and they shot him dead, in front of his wife. She was lucky that they didn't kill her as well. Who knows which side they were on?

Once only, between 1939 and 1941, Władysław dared to travel from Truskawiec to Lwów to see how Łucja and Julian were faring. Even that journey was fraught with danger for all of them. He was a target and his family would have been targeted through him. Therefore the journey had to be in secret. He would, as Julian wrote, have had to avoid both Dziedziłow and Meryszczów, because the Russians were systematically arresting, deporting to Russia and imprisoning all Polish landowners. When he came back to Lwów, for that last visit, he had been working as a lorry driver in Borysław where there were oilfields, not too far from Truskawiec. Julian, now aged fourteen and well aware of what was going on, suspected that Rozalia had relatives in this area who may have helped them, but her name was never mentioned within his hearing. It must have been a sad and stressful meeting. I can only imagine the conversations, the debates, the plans that were made and abandoned, the solutions that couldn't be found. My father never wrote more than a few sad paragraphs about it, and Władysław headed south again, without any firm strategy as to what they could do to protect themselves, other than continue to keep a low profile and hope for the best.

It couldn't last.

Władysław was denounced to the Soviets, by whom it is not recorded, although it's tempting to guess, arrested in Truskawiec and imprisoned. He was moved to the notorious Kharkiv prison in Ukraine, which was under Russian occupation. From there we can assume he was sent to a Gulag, but I don't know which one and records are silent or destroyed. The Soviets regarded captured Polish military personnel as counter-revolutionaries, and not prisoners-of-war. This gave them carte blanche to do whatever they wanted with these people, including cold blooded murder. The USSR had not signed the Geneva Convention, nor did it recognise the Hague Convention on the treatment of POWs and I doubt if it would have made any difference if they had. The Red Cross were not allowed to supervise their treatment. Prisoners were handed over to the NKVD, otherwise known as the secret police, and convicted of treason to Russia. This essentially allowed for their extermination in whatever way Stalin liked. Putin seems to be following the same doctrine in Ukraine. The

NKVD took control of Polish prisoners and organised a network of transit camps so as to facilitate transporting these prisoners to work camps in the USSR. These included not just serving soldiers, but boy scouts, police and prison officers as well as writers and academics who would have been seen as a threat to the regime.

One of these camps was in the infamous Katyn forest.

A report in November 1939 stated that the NKVD were holding, even then, some 40,000 Poles, but that was followed by more arrests in December of that year and in succeeding years. In these camps the Poles were subject to relentless interrogation. They were promised that they would be released if they displayed the correct political sentiments, but in effect their captors were deciding who would live and who would die. Most of them were deemed to be enemies of Soviet authority, which was a capital offence. In March 1940, Stalin signed an order for the execution of 'nationalists and counter revolutionaries', which resulted among other things in the notorious Katyn Massacre, the blanket name given to a series of mass executions of the Polish officer corps or as many as they could lay their hands on. 22,000 Polish officers were murdered in cold blood. Of the total killed, about 8000 had been imprisoned during the 1939 Soviet invasion. There were some 6,000 police officers, and the remaining 8,000 were loosely dubbed 'the intelligentsia' a catch-all term for those whom the Soviets deemed to be spies or potential saboteurs: landowners, factory owners, lawyers, officials, artists, writers, musicians, actors and priests. The Polish Army officer class was representative of what had been a multi-ethnic Polish state, albeit one with occasional unrest. Those murdered included ethnic Poles, Ukrainians, Belarusians and Jews, including the chief Rabbi of the Polish army. Władysław escaped execution. He had been imprisoned as *szlachta* rather than an army officer, so was sent to a Gulag, a forced labour camp, or into a punishment battalion instead. Many Poles were sent into these battalions, which would mean almost certain death for people already debilitated by prison, starvation and forced labour.

Meanwhile, the Russian soldiers had also arrived in Tatarów. At this point, although many Poles left, Wanda and Karol elected to stay on for the time being, while keeping open the option to leave. Yet again, it must have been difficult to decide what to do. Although Karol had fought and been injured in WW1, he was manifestly not in the army now. Wanda tended to her garden and grew her vegetables and had none of the hallmarks of the enemy. Stalin was no friend to the Polish intelligentsia, but the Russian soldiers that did arrive were, as Teresa wrote, 'in poor shape' and seemed less threatening here than in the rest of Galicia. Although most of the guest houses were subject to nationalisation, and divided into single rooms to house the workers, Karol was surprised to be told that he would have some small privileges as an artist – mainly because Stalin rather liked some of his and his two famous forebears' paintings. If this seems surprising, because so many of Juliusz and Wojciech's paintings involved battles against the Russians, I suppose the fact that the subjects were

Tsarist Russians may have helped. Nevertheless, the guest house took in lodgers during this period and at least some of them would have been Poles who had tried and failed to get over the border into Romania or Hungary, including a man named Zdzisław Jankowski whom they had known from pre-war days.

Teresa writes, 'For my parents and for me, the Russian occupation was not so much tragic as hard. They were poor, cold and hungry for much of the time and people in this situation don't want to buy art. Besides, paint and paper were in short supply. Wanda's fruit and vegetables were a godsend, but eventually, they had to sell their wedding rings to pay for food.'

Reading accounts of this time from people such as Teresa, it strikes me how, even in the middle of potentially desperate situations, where any moment the world will come crumbling down around your ears, people will carry on with their day to day lives as best they can. When there is nothing else to be done, you just get on with things. They worked, they foraged, and they did the best they could to survive.

In Lwów under Russian occupation, food was also very scarce, so fourteen year old Julian used to go back to Dziedziłow, in search of provisions for himself, his mother and her sister. When he arrived there, he found that his childhood home was occupied by a Soviet party official, so Julian always went in secret and stayed with his nanny, Marysia. She and her husband had been reconciled with her parents and the family were all living together on their small farm. Jósef Szwagulak, for all that he professed to be a Ukrainian Bolshevik, never gave his young friend away.

In fact, Julian wrote that all these people were generous with whatever food they had and offered him love, comfort and hospitality in spite of the risk to themselves. During these visits, he would sneak around the estate, curious to see what had happened to it. He was always accompanied by Jósef so that he could pretend to be a relative, in case of any challenge to his presence there. One of the things that saddened him most, was to see that the 300 year old linden had been cut down. It seemed to stand for all that had been swept away, all the unnecessary carnage. Some of the family furniture had been taken (or rescued?) from the house, and in one case at least, the earth floor of a cottage had been dug out to make room for the carved wooden sideboard, the same sideboard from which Danuta had pinched food for their midnight feasts less than a decade earlier. Calfskin from his father's books had been used for shoe leather. But needs must, said my philosophical father, and everyone was suffering bitterly under Russian occupation.

Julian had travelled on one of these food gathering expeditions in 1941, staying in Dziedziłow for two or three weeks, when war broke out between the Russians and the Germans. He wasn't to know it, but this would have been a potential turning point for his father, many miles away in the East.

'There wasn't a huge amount of fighting, but after two or three days, it was suddenly as though the whole area was under German occupation,' he wrote.

As indeed it was.

I think, here in the UK, which has seen no genuine occupation since the Normans, we have no idea at all about the swiftness and suddenness with which these things can happen, and how easy it can be to be caught up in having entirely the wrong nominal allegiance, speaking the wrong language, having the wrong papers. Once again, dreadfully worried about his mother and aunt, he decided that he must get back to the city as soon as possible, and hauled a suitcase full of cheese, ham, fruit and vegetables, across the thirty miles to Lwów. Imagine how difficult it must have been for a boy to keep himself and his precious cargo of provisions safe, not knowing what he would encounter around the next bend in the road.

'Every so often, I managed to get a lift in a farm cart for a few miles, but for the rest of the time I walked.'

Dad never liked to go into graphic details about that journey. Those who do revel in such things, or who like to pontificate about them and what people 'should have done', have hardly ever experienced them. But he remarked, almost casually, that it was a gruesome journey along main roads littered with mutilated bodies from both sides of the fight, partisans who had come down on one side or another, Russian and German, Ukrainian and Pole, people who had lived together and married but were now sworn enemies. I've often wondered what became of Marynia's Józef. My father thought that perhaps Paulina hadn't survived the war, but how would he know? There were a few other people he assumed had been killed but who had in fact survived – displaced, traumatised, but alive. On this occasion, the Russians retreated fairly rapidly in the countryside, but there had been a lot more resistance in Lwów where they had become entrenched. When Julian got back to their apartment, he found that, as he put it with masterly understatement, 'Łucja and her sister had not had an easy time,' so he was glad to be back, even if his city was now under Hitler's General Government.

CHAPTER SEVENTEEN

German Occupation

In 1941, the uneasy liaison between Stalin and Hitler came to an end and war broke out between the Germans and the Russians, a fact celebrated by the Allies, but provoking a less than comfortable state of affairs for those again caught between the Russian rock and the hard place of Nazi Germany. In June 1941, the Soviets were in retreat, and now the German supporting Hungarians came to Tatarów where the Kossaks, Wanda, Karol and Teresa, were just about managing to survive. The Hungarians who came were reasonably civilised, wrote Teresa, and for a while there was a certain amount of reassurance. After all, not so long ago, they had all been part of the same Hapsburg Empire. This small spell of stability didn't last and when the committed Nazis arrived, everything suddenly got infinitely worse for all of them, but worst of all for the Jewish population.

The Kossaks had a Jewish friend called Mr Popiel, and before the Nazis arrived, Wanda had hidden his family silverware for him. The Gestapo accused her of the serious crime of 'hiding Jewish Property'. All such property was being confiscated. Both Wanda and Karol were taken in for interrogation, not once but several times, while their lodger, Mr Jankowski, looked after Teresa. They never saw Mr Popiel again. Few Poles and Ukrainians now remained in Tatarów and the Kossak family too began making plans to leave, without knowing where to go. Teresa remembered another friend of the family, an elderly Jewish trader in wood, called Mr Chaim. He was elegant, smart and charming, and he was one of the first victims of the incoming Nazis. The Kossaks survived, given a little latitude because, like Stalin, the Führer also thought of himself as an artist, a fact best commemorated in the satirical film The Producers. But Karol's work too could be satirical, and he was not known for keeping a low profile where his art was concerned. Some of his work during these years was so subversive that it would, if known to the Nazis, have merited imprisonment and probably death. The Hucul wedding parties were safer. Perhaps that was why he came to hate them so much.

What had happened to Władysław in the meantime? I was helped in my research by two gentlemen, both named Tadeusz Czerkawski, distant relatives, war heroes, one living in Poland and one in London, both sadly no longer with us. The English based 'Ted' called me not long after my father's death and gave me a shock by the way in which he sounded exactly like my father, not just because of his Polish accent, but because he had precisely the same timbre of voice so it was like getting a call from my much missed Dad. When I had recovered my equilibrium, we had a long chat. He himself had bitter knowledge of that time and place. Between the three of us, the two Teds and myself, we managed to piece together what had become of my grandfather.

'And now about your grandfather, Władysław,' he writes. 'Certainly, he was in Kharkiv prison. I had been there too in February 1941. But Kharkiv was normally a place of temporary imprisonment. That is, in that prison, we Poles, condemned to anything from three to ten years and more in the Gulags, waited in terrible conditions for transport to these forced labour camps.'

My grandfather went from Kharkiv prison to an unknown Gulag, but which one that might have been, I've been unable to determine, and records are few and far between. What none of his close family knew was that early in 1942, Władysław had been released, after a fashion. This was not a liberation, as Tadeusz points out, since there were extreme constraints on the conditions.

'A Polish citizen was not liberated from a Gulag. But after the so-called amnesty of autumn 1941 these (mostly) men were enlisted in the Polish army in the East. Many Polish soldiers died of illness and deprivation during this terrible period which seems only to have involved a change from forced labour to forced travel. So Władysław left whichever labour camp he had been in, to join the Polish Army in the East, more popularly known as General Anders' Army. It was a long, long trek.'

'The old town of Bukhara, on the silk road, and the capital of Tamerlaine's empire, is situated in Uzbekistan, 250 kilometres north of the Afghanistan frontier,' writes Tadeusz. It is a name with a certain romance about it. 'Kenimech or Kenimekh is a town 75 kilometres to the North-east of Bukhara. Mirbazar is a village among many others, around Kenimekh. To those villages came various

Polish military units. Those of the seventh infantry division came to Kermine which was very close to Kenimekh.'

According to Władysław's Ministry of Defence war record, which was maintained because he was officially part of General Anders' army, a mortally ill Władysław arrived at Kermine on 4th June, 1942, and died on 30th July, 1942, at the age of thirty-eight. He is buried at Mirbazar. In the meantime, his son, Julian, was struggling to help provide for his mother and aunt in Lwów, as well as doing whatever he could to help the anti-Nazi resistance.

As Tadeusz told me, 'Two months ago, I got a very important book. It is Piotr Zaron's Eastern Direction in General Władysław Sikorski's military-political strategy, 1940–43.' The author writes about Polish-Soviet relations in those years and the organisation of the Polish army in the East under General Anders' command. The book has an appendix, a register of soldiers of the Polish army who died in the Soviet Union from September 1941 to September 1942, among which we find:

Lancer Czerkawski, Władysław: born 14th January 1904, Przemyślany (Meryszczów) voy Tarnopolskie, died 30th July 1942 in Mirbazar, Kenimech, Buried Mirbazar Military Cemetery Row 165, Tomb 1.

More recent research reveals that the cemetery has been tidied up and rationalised to some extent, with a single monument to all the people buried there, but it seems to be reasonably well kept now.

'It is impossible to say exactly what your grandfather would have died of,' writes Tadeusz. 'Typhoid, malaria, dysentery or sheer exhaustion. Half hour ago, I telephoned my friend, Lancer George Dochkal, living in Warsaw. He had been a soldier in Kenimech in 1942. He described a period of terrible epidemic amoebic dysentery. The mortality was so high, that the grave diggers had to work day and night to bury dead Polish soldiers in the newly constructed Polish military cemetery.'

The truth was that these people had arrived at army reception camps in Tashkent, Kermine, Samarkand and Ashkhabad, where very little provision had been made for them. Stalin detested them. It was bad enough for these debilitated soldiers, for whom at least there were reception camps. But there were also hundreds of thousands of exiled women and children, who were camped outside in chaotic conditions, sick, starving and with few resources or even hopes, other than to keep going East to possible freedom. Instead of increasing provisions to the camps to account for them, the Soviets deliberately cut them. In response, those desperate Polish officers who had survived began to enlist civilians including women and children into the army ranks, by whatever means possible. This was essentially to give them some, any, military status, to save them from starvation. Bureaucracy is often more regarded than human life in these situations, as we recently saw all too clearly in Afghanistan and as we are seeing with Ukrainian refugees.

Władysław has been very much on my mind as I write this, almost eighty years later. He was thirty-eight. Two years older than my own son. He had once had the world at his feet. He had a son he loved very much, and whose inheritance it was clear that he had wished to secure. He would not have known whether that son had survived, nor what had become of his wife or the other woman in his life. What was his state of mind at this time? He was brave, funny, charming, mercurial, intelligent and doomed. Without ever knowing the answer to any of the hideous fears and worries that must have beset him, he died of fever, chills, bloody diarrhoea and intense abdominal pain at the hottest time of the year and was buried in Mirbazar not far from the Silk Road.

He was by no means alone. Epidemic diseases were running rampant, and as Tadeusz's friend pointed out, the gravediggers could not keep up with the numbers who were dying. By 1942, a scant half of the almost two million Polish citizens arrested by the Soviets at the start of the war were still alive. Their salvation finally came when Stalin was persuaded to evacuate some of the Polish forces to Iran, with a small number of civilians accompanying them. Among those who finally made it to Iran, was Władysław's brother-in-law, Feliks. His wife, Ludmiła was not so lucky. She had been living in Warsaw and so fell into the hands of the Nazis.

The rest, even after the defeat of the Nazis and the liberation of the German camps on Polish soil, had to stay behind and face their fate as reluctant Soviet citizens, a state of affairs which persisted for many years after the war was over for most of Western Europe. Even here in Britain, the new British Labour government, to their everlasting shame, submitted to pressure from Stalin and did not invite the Polish Armed Forces, not even the airmen who had fought in the Battle of Britain, to the 1946 Victory Parade in London. I wonder what my anglophile grandfather would have thought about that? I know that my father, who voted Labour all his life, once he was naturalised and able to vote, still despised them for it, as do I.

In April 1943, in Tatarów, the Kossak house had suffered a dreadful fire. A Ukrainian chimney sweep got the blame, but Teresa doubted if it was more than a tragic accident. Wooden houses burn all too easily. Sadly, although they rescued some of their possessions, many of Karol's pictures did not survive. The destruction of their home, along with the increasing brutality of the Nazis, finally made them decide to move somewhere, anywhere. But where? Nowhere was safe. People travelled to get away from something and often ran straight into trouble elsewhere.

They decided first of all to go to Stanisławow (now Ivano Frankivsk) eighty kilometres north of Tatarów, intending to try to make the long journey north west to Jasło, which Karol knew from his youth, and thence to Bączal where he was born. This would involve a journey of almost five hundred kilometres by slow train. He was anxious to see what had become of the other members of his family there and in Warsaw. In Stanisławow, little Teresa fell ill with pneumonia, and it was only through the goodwill of an officer in the Wehrmacht, who turned out to be an old college friend of Karol's from Vienna, that they managed to get some precious medicine for her. Once more, I reflect how difficult it is for British people, with their very fixed perceptions of the war, to understand this kind of interaction. Karol would have spent time in Vienna, would have made many friends there, would probably have corresponded with them until war made such friendships precarious. Poland had been part of the Austro-Hungarian Empire for many years. The Wehrmacht were not the Gestapo. Some of them were young men caught up in a conflict not of their making or desiring.

There followed a long and painful journey on a very slow train, starting and stopping every few kilometres. Wanda had packed up as much as they could carry. They had brought anything that looked as though it could be exchanged for cash or food, including candlesticks from Meryszczów, and a few pictures. Teresa remembered gazing at a boundless landscape of meadows and plains, during this long journey of stops and starts. At one halt, Karol, who had disembarked for a few moments to relieve himself, disappeared, and the train started without him. She described the acute panic and her mother's frantic prayers. Two days later, a little further down the line, he reappeared when the train stopped again, traumatised and drunk. Parties of Nazi soldiers were randomly picking up whichever Poles they could find at stations, and compelling them at gunpoint to bury the bodies of murdered Jews, after which they would release them wherever they could catch up with the train, a small mercy among so much brutality. They had forced raw spirits down their prisoners' throats to anaesthetise them against the horror of what they had witnessed, a horror that had rendered most of them speechless and almost immobile until numbed with alcohol.

In or near *Jasło*, where again Karol produced anti-Nazi sketches full of the revulsion and inhumanity he had experienced, they were surprised to meet Niobcia, Bogusław's wife, and her sister. It was here that a traumatised Wanda learned of her brother's fate. She also learned the terrible news that her younger sister, Ludmiła, had been denounced as the wife of a senior army officer, arrested by the Nazis in Warsaw and sent to a concentration camp, where nothing had been heard of her since. Teresa notes that Niobcia had acquired a local admirer, somebody she had known from the house parties of her youth. He helped them to find food and medicine, but times were precarious and they were again running out of things to sell. By now, the Russians were advancing again, the front was approaching and this time the Russian army seemed to be in better shape than before. Josep Bandera's Ukrainian nationalists were in the woods. Perils were everywhere, but at least the Germans were in retreat.

Still, it felt, said Teresa later, as though they were 'mice under a broom', a characteristically graphic description.

In Lwów, meanwhile, Julian, his mother and aunt were also 'mice under a broom'. They were unaware of Władysław's death, although they must have feared the worst, knowing only that he would have disappeared into the Siberian wastes, a knowledge that was all my father had until many years later when, with the help of a number of Polish relatives and friends, I finally discovered the truth.

I have my father's identity card from the time of the German occupation of Lwów. This is dated 30th May 1944 when Dad would have been just eighteen, which probably explains the new registration. It is supposed to last till

May 1949. When I was applying to regain my own Polish nationality, a pleasant Polish diplomat glanced at this with raised eyebrows. 'Hmm. *They* were optimistic!' he said, wryly. On this card, Lwów is back to its old Austro-Hungarian name of Lemberg. Julian, his mother and aunt are living at Schillerstrasse 45. It is a sad and battered little document. It gives his place of birth as Dziedziłow, handy when I came to reclaim my Polish nationality, and even the postal address of the house there, in German of course: Kamionka Strasse. His religion is Roman Catholic, he has no 'special characteristics' but his occupation is recorded as locksmith or metal worker. There is a page of closely written instructions and warnings about this essential document. There is a head and shoulders photograph of my young father wearing a shirt and tie under what looks like an overall jacket. And there are his fingerprints.

'Under German Occupation, I still went to Dziedziłow and also to Meryszczów to get some provisions, travelling there several times, during 1942 and 1943,' wrote my father. 'In Dziedziłow, I again stayed with Marynia and Józef Szwagulak, and people who had once benefited from my father's generosity were generous in return, giving me whatever supplies they could spare. In Meryszczów, surprisingly, I stayed in the big house, with the estate manager who had been employed by my father before the war. The estate was in good shape now, even though it was run for the benefit of the German occupation powers. There was a herd of dairy cattle with plenty of horses and quite a lot of market gardening. They were growing soft fruit, tomatoes and other vegetables. In fact I could tell that the estate was in better shape than it had been for many years, although of course it was all for the benefit of the Nazis and not for the Polish inhabitants.' I found this observation more than a little poignant, especially in view of the sense of desolation encountered by Teresa Kossak and her friend during their 2007 trip to the same place, with its green landscape, but also with its failed collective farm, recalling postwar drought, famine and the terrors of the Stalinist era. And now there's Putin's war.

There was no more school for Poles in German occupied Lwów. Or as my father put it, 'no such thing for Polish slaves!' There was only primary school, which was as much as they would need for the menial tasks that were to be their lot in the great empire of Hitler's warped imagination. His aim was nothing less than the total destruction of the Polish state and the enslavement of its inhabitants. In 1942, therefore, sixteen year old Julian, with a good basic knowledge of growing things, went to work as a gardener, but also, in spite of his mother's protests, joined the covert resistance movement or Home Army. He was still her 'beloved little Julian' and she was desperately worried for him, although like all young men, and in spite of all evidence to the contrary, he probably believed himself immortal.

'Half of it was like a game,' he wrote. 'People were deliberately given things to do to keep their spirits up, even by the Resistance.'

Like all wars, times of extreme terror were interspersed with long periods of extreme boredom when nothing whatsoever could be done to change things and you just survived as best you could. Julian worked as a plumber for a while, and then the Home Army instructed him to join a German building firm, ostensibly to train as a locksmith. He was always practical, always good with his hands, and although he eventually became a research scientist, he always had the strong hands of a working man, with oil or dust so deeply ingrained that it could seldom be washed off without scrubbing. My mother used to complain about it, albeit not very vociferously, since in her heart she was very proud of him. I grew up with a father who could fix anything, and it coloured my view of the world ever afterwards.

The German building firm, which seems to have been a reasonably civilised outfit, sent people to work all over the country. This meant that the young people working for them could and did act as covert couriers. Julian was instructed to carry messages to the Resistance in southern Ukraine. He travelled as far as Yalta, the resort on the Crimean Peninsula where two or three years later, in 1945, Poland's fate would be sealed by the Big Three of Roosevelt, Churchill and Stalin. Julian travelled ostensibly on lock making business, with a packet of papers sewn into his jacket, exchanged the jacket for a substitute, and came home by goods train, travelling with a group of rather fine horses, probably requisitioned by the Germans. These journeys became so routine that the young people involved ignored the very real dangers of discovery and death. Soon, the Germans were beginning to withdraw and 'everyone was going home if they could'.

In spite of the fact that the estate at Meryszczów was thriving in an economic sense, horrible things were happening in and around the village, often involving the

Organisation of Ukrainian Nationalists and their adherents. Further East in Ukraine, ethnic cleansing was carried out by the Ukrainian Insurgent Army with the support of some of the local population, and this spilled over elsewhere. Most of the massacres took place during July and August of 1943, and involved mainly women and children who were tortured before being murdered. This resulted in between 50,000 and 100,000 deaths. As Timothy Snyder writes in his fine account *Bloodlands*, which is required, though very difficult, reading, this was a vicious Ukrainian attempt to prevent any post war Polish state from reasserting its sovereignty over those areas that had previously been part of Poland.

They were linked to Stepan Bandera's Ukrainian Insurgent Army who wanted to purge all non-Ukrainians from the area. This, of course, led to retaliation by the Polish Home Army, albeit on a smaller scale. Bandera, celebrated by some and detested by others, had been born in Galicia as part of the family of an Orthodox priest. He quarrelled with the authorities, became radicalised and eventually threw in his lot with Hitler. He was and remains a deeply controversial figure. It would be true to say that for those who didn't like his principles, he could always find a different set. He was assassinated in Munich in 1959, allegedly by a KGB defector. The wartime fate of his entire family is as horrific as you would expect, and he remains to this day a divisive figure in Ukraine.

In 2016 the Polish Parliament described the Volhynia and other Galician massacres as genocide, although some non-Polish historians dispute this and call it 'ethnic cleansing' as though this were somehow less morally and actually sickening. Where does ethnic cleansing end and genocide begin? Where does hatred of one group of people for another group of people, to the extent that they can be tortured and killed for the accident of their birth, ever become anything less than evil? We begin with whataboutery and excuses for 'othering' a group of people, and we end with unimaginable horrors. It isn't as though it hasn't happened before. It isn't as though we can plead ignorance of what is possible in such a situation. In a publication called The Barbarism of the OUN-UPA, in 2009, Jósef Wyspiański describes in graphic and distressing detail, the horrific torture and burning to death of an elderly Polish woman just outside Meryszczów, watched and applauded by a number of people. Was this ethnic cleansing? Does disputing the terminology of this contribute anything useful to the debate? Can't we just condemn it as the unforgivable brutality it is and try to prevent it from ever happening again? Or is that, as seems ever more likely now, an impossible dream?

After his time as a courier for the Home Army, and with the Nazis beleaguered on many fronts, Julian joined the Resistance in the woods near Warsaw. When he left his mother and aunt in Lwów, neither of them would have known that he and his mother would not meet again for fifteen years and that Lwów would soon no longer be a Polish city, that in 1945, the NKVD, the Soviet secret police, would arrest thousands of Poles, to 'encourage the others' to head west. Julian was in Warsaw when the Uprising started in August 1944. He never spoke about this time at all, except to say that he had been there, but most Poles will agree that it was a brave attempt that should have succeeded, but was scuppered by the Allies, mostly in the shape of the Red Army. Anna Danuta Hanakowska was also in Warsaw at this time, working as a messenger or a nurse, but my father was unaware of it.

The Uprising was supposed to liberate Warsaw from the Nazis and had been deliberately timed to coincide as precisely as possible with the retreat of the German army occupying the city, just ahead of the advancing Russians. It should have worked. At the Eastern suburbs of Warsaw, the Red Army stopped combat operations, thus allowing the Germans time to regroup and defeat the Polish resistance. Historians have debated the reasons why, but the Poles fought on for sixty-three days, with no outside support from their so called allies at all. It was the biggest military effort made by any European resistance movement, and it failed because of what was perceived as a deliberate decision by Russia to throw Warsaw to the wolves. Not only did the Germans regroup and defeat the Uprising, but they then went on to destroy the city itself as an act of brutal retaliation. It was a lesson to the Poles with what those same Poles saw as the tacit approval of the Russians. As anyone who has seen reconnaissance film of the time knows, this was a beautiful historic city that was destroyed not by bombing from above, but literally razed to the ground by deliberately placed explosives from below. That it has been largely and determinedly rebuilt is a testament to human defiance in the face of iniquity.

CHAPTER EIGHTEEN

Reconnecting

Many years after the war, the first person from his old life that Julian managed to get in touch with was his mother, Łucja, after whom I had my middle name. I was Catherine because of my mother's love for Wuthering Heights and Lucy for my grandmother. This was in the very late fifties or early sixties, through the good offices of the Red Cross, which was still trying to reunite displaced families. Łucja had survived the war, and was living with her sister, Nusia, in an industrial town called Wałbrzych. She had been forced to leave Lwów, which had been handed over to Russia by three powerful men in Yalta. There is some evidence that Roosevelt in particular was indifferent and unwilling to resist Stalin on this point. The mass arrests of Poles in Lwów had lasted until January 1945, with some 17,000 Poles, including scientists, engineers, artists and especially anyone who had been in the Home Army being detained by the secret police. The intention had been to 'encourage' the rest to leave. It worked. I don't know when Łucja and her sister left their Lwów apartment, but they never saw it again, and they took almost nothing with them.

She saw her son once more, when Julian managed to obtain permission for her to visit us in Leeds, a tricky process for anyone who wanted to travel from east to west. She had been a cheerfully pampered girl and was now a sad and embittered lady in her sixties, looking much older than her years. My parents did their best to make her stay a happy one, but I don't think she liked Leeds and she certainly didn't want to stay there. She had expected more of it, more of us. She was beset by arthritis, miserable and very sad. The discrepancy between her beloved little Julek in his velvet suit, or even the brave eighteen year old Julian who had waved goodbye to her, going off to join the Warsaw resistance, and the grown up husband and father she met so many years later must have been very difficult if not impossible for her to come to terms with, as it would have been hard for almost anyone. He was a time traveller, whose Polish sounded oddly dated. He had an English speaking wife and a shy little English speaking daughter, and they lived in a chilly urban flat with paraffin heaters and few luxuries. Perhaps she had expected more of the west.

Times were even harder in communist Poland, especially for women working in tobacco kiosks, which was the only employment Łucja had been able to find, and Mum and Dad sent regular parcels of food, toiletries and such medicines as were available. I still remember them being carefully packaged up, the long and very precisely detailed lists needed for Customs, and the hope that items wouldn't be stolen along the way, as they occasionally were. I think about her more and more these days. I was a child when I met her. To me, back then, she seemed old, querulous and cross. But I also think about her as a pretty young woman in Lwów, meeting her handsome Władysław at a ball or house party and being charmed by him. I think about her expectations back then, her obvious love for her son, and the way in which everything came crashing down around her ears. The chaos of those times. Her rage at Rozalia and at the husband who had betrayed her. Her bitterness over lost dreams and dashed hopes. Her loneliness. Some coped better than others, but it's hard to blame anyone for losing heart. Which of us can say that we would not have lost heart too?

A happier meeting was with Wanda and Karol Kossak who were still, more or less contentedly, settled in Ciechocinek. Wanda was more satisfied with her life than Łucja, but then she hadn't lost quite so much. And perhaps she had been less demanding to begin with. A manager. A survivor. I can't now remember whether Łucja put them in touch with my father or whether it was another contact facilitated by the Red Cross, but they corresponded regularly, my parents sent parcels of precious art materials to Ciechocinek, and when it became possible, my mother and father visited them there, and spent time with Teresa and her partner Andrzej in Warsaw and at Lipki, Andrzej's picturesque family summer house in the forest. I went there too, and picked mushrooms with them in the autumn, wandering through the forests with a basket in the way that my forebears had done, bringing them back for Teresa to examine carefully in case any of them were poisonous.

When I stayed with my Kossak relations in 1974, they welcomed me and gave me an enticing flavour of the Poland they had not quite lost. Teresa's small apartment in a Warsaw tower block seemed to me the very height of sophistication. She had followed in her family's artistic footsteps and was an animator, working among other projects on the popular Polish 'Lolek i Bolek' cartoons. The flat was full of textiles, artworks and her collection of individual porcelain cups and saucers, mostly bought in flea markets, out of which we drank strong black tea. She seemed very beautiful to me. I can still picture her elegance, her slightly husky voice, her careful way of moving, her generosity to me. She smoked, she drank more shots of vodka than my mother (and, I'm sure, her mother too) would have thought wise, and she had a group of fascinating friends: artists, writers, museum curators, photographers, silversmiths, somebody who worked in amber. I visited his amber studio and he showed me how the resin was polished, and how the process released the scent of a thousand ancient forests into the studio.

'I would get more commissions if I joined the Party,' he said. 'But I won't.'

He was old enough to have taken part in the Warsaw Uprising. He took me for a walk around the Old Town on a cold evening, the lamps just lit, the sky a dark, wintry blue, frost sparkling on stones.

'I see ghosts of my friends on every corner,' he said. He made me see them too.

For quite some time, I wanted to *be* Teresa, and there is some small part of me that still does. Most of all, I think she and Andrzej, who was as briskly charming and funny as only an old fashioned Pole can be, and with whom I was half in love, brought the past alive for me in a way that no amount of reading ever can.

In 1978, I spent a year at Wrocław University, teaching English conversation, on a lectureship sponsored by the

British Council. That Christmas, after being persuaded to sing White Christmas for a class of ninety young people, I went to visit my surviving family in Warsaw: Teresa, Andrzej, and Wanda, widowed for three years, travelling to the city from Ciechocinek. We were guests at the busy Kossak family house at Żoliborz, a suburb of the city that had largely survived the Nazi destruction, and I was carried back in time to a traditional Polish Christmas Eve supper, begun when the first star is in the sky, a supper with many meatless courses and again, copious amounts of vodka. My memory of that evening is a blur of eating, drinking, Christmas carols and chatter in Polish, English and French, especially from the older members of the family for whom France had been a place of style and culture. There were excited children and older friends and relatives, voluble in several languages at once. Throughout the whole celebration, their pet tortoise clattered about the polished parquet floor. It still stands out in my memory as a glimpse of a culture that was mine and yet not mine. I think it was probably then that I first realised that I was, in fact, a citizen of nowhere, a European if I was anything, and it was fine by me. A good identity to recognise in myself.

It was in Wrocław that I met a Czerkawski cousin who told me what had become of my grandfather's sister, Ludmiła Machnowska. She had fallen foul of the Nazis, as the wife of a Polish officer, and had been arrested and sent to a concentration camp. Towards the end of the war, they had both been in the same camp, Belsen. Ludka had probably been transferred from Auschwitz. As the Allies advanced, the Nazis marched prisoners from other camps to Belsen so that their numbers swelled from 7300 to some 60,000. Tens of thousands of people died along the way and in the camp itself. She survived until the end of the war, but deprivation and sickness had taken its toll, and just before liberation, she died without ever knowing what had become of her husband. I think she would have assumed that he was dead.

Against all the odds, Feliks Machnowski survived the war. He had been arrested by the Soviets and deported deep into the USSR. He was lucky not to be murdered. As it turned out, it would have been marginally better for Ludmiła if she had been deported alongside him. It might at least have given her a small chance of survival. Like my grandfather, he too was released to join General Anders' army but unlike Władysław, he survived. He managed to make his way to Tehran, where he was colonel in command of the evacuation centre for the families of soldiers who had served in the USSR. From there, he travelled through the Middle East and in the Italian campaign he partic-ipated in the battle of Monte Cassino. After December 1944, he found himself in Peebles, here in Scotland, as a lecturer at the Polish War College. It was here that he must have learned of Ludmiła's death, because in the UK Polish language newspaper, we find an announcement for a memorial service for 'Ludwiki Machnowskiej of the Czerkawski family, to be held on the 25th October, 1945, at 9am, in the Catholic church in Peebles.' The sad little notice, bordered in black, indicates that she died in Belsen in April of that same year. It must surely have struck him that a few months more and they might have been reunited.

Or perhaps not. Like all concentration camps, Belsen was a hell hole, a place that even Hieronymus Bosch would have found hard to depict in all its terrible reality. Even a few moments searching online reveals ghastly photographs of the scenes that met those who liberated this place. So horrific, that the brain refuses to process them, refuses to believe that these skeletal assemblages of arms, legs, torsos, heads can ever have been human beings. It was the camp where Anne Frank died of typhus, and I think Ludmiła contracted the same sickness. It was a camp already riven with disease, to which the diseased were sent to die. The traumatised liberators, having taken out the survivors, had to bury the dead in mass graves and burn the rest of it to the ground, not just to kill the organisms causing disease, but an act, somehow, of purification. Richard Dimbleby described the scene there shortly after liberation. The BBC originally refused to play the broadcast, unable to believe the horror, or unwilling to process it, but after he threatened to resign, they did.

'Dead bodies, some of them in decay, lay strewn about the road and along the rutted tracks ... Inside the huts it was even worse. The dead and the dying lay close together. I picked my way over corpse after corpse, until I heard one voice above the gentle moaning. I found a girl. She was a living skeleton. Impossible to gauge her age, for she had practically no hair left on her head, and her face was only a yellow parchment sheet, with two holes in it for eyes.'

Now, there is a Bergen Belsen website, solemn, low key and informative, with graceful responses to emails, an object lesson in how to cope with a terrible legacy that can't be obliterated by ignoring or denying the reality of it. When I was teaching in Poland, one of my mature students was a kindly engineer who came from a place called Oświęcim. 'Auschwitz,' he said. And then, a little sadly, 'somebody has to come from there. And it was once a nice little town you know. Before the Nazis.' Everyone I have ever known who experienced the war in all its horror has been remarkably silent about it. This is mostly because – in the same way that returning soldiers from WW1 couldn't begin to describe the Trenches to their loved ones – it was impossible for them to put their experiences into words. They knew that almost every depiction of it was wrong or inadequate, but they couldn't begin to correct that inadequacy. The people who are all too happy to use it for their own political ends were never there and don't seem to have the imagination to perceive that they too may have participated in unimaginable horrors, given a similar situation. My father knew it. My grandfather would have known it. Obedience and complacency can be killers. Who among us, even now, dares to stand up for what we believe to be right in the face of psychological antagonism, let alone physical danger?

I can't bear to think of Ludmiła, of my grandfather's funny, elegant sister, buried without any monument to her existence. At least my grandfather had that, a record of his identity. There is the memorial service organised by her husband. There is her name and place of birth, written in a book of remembrance at the museum for the camp, and I am told that her grave is known, but there is no individual monument to her. So many had to be buried together.

Does she rest in peace there? I hope so.

Feliks Machnowski remained in Scotland for some years, but in January 1948 he married a local woman called Margaret Sinclair Leutfoot, the daughter of a retired baker. They were married in St John's Roman Catholic Church in Perth. I have a copy of their marriage certificate here, which gives me the surprising information that the father of such a stylish war hero had been an inspector for the Polish Inland Revenue, although there is no reason at all why tax inspector fathers should not have heroic sons. Eventually the couple emigrated to Argentina, which was where Feliks died in 1966, only a little while after we too had moved to Scotland.

Against all the odds, Władysław's sister, Danuta Hanakowska, also survived. Back in early 2020, when the seriousness of the Covid pandemic was becoming apparent, I began to collate all the years of research that I had done, with this project in mind. There is a huge box full of paperwork, photocopies, pictures, documents and my father's precious handwritten accounts. Tucked away among those papers was a handwritten letter in Polish from Jerzy Hanakowski, Jan Hanakowski's son from his second marriage, after Anna's death. There were two problems with it. One was that it was sent in 2002 (coincidentally, on my father's birthday, 24th May) but Dad had died in 1995, and at that time, I didn't know anyone who could translate it for me. That was not an insurmountable problem in itself, but the other was more difficult. There was no return address.

Nor could I find one anywhere among the many papers, that included various envelopes I'd preserved. I had other more pressing work on at the time, so I had clearly filed it away and forgotten all about it until 2020 and this project. A Polish friend, Iwona Piasecka, translated it for me and she was as intrigued as I was. Not only did Jerzy give me some fascinating information about his relationship with my grandfather, but he also told me that although his elder sister was no longer alive, she had survived the war, and had gone to the USA as a nurse, in 1946. He told me that he loved my grandfather so much that he named his first son Władysław in his honour. And then Jerzy in old age was threatened by the same brutal invaders who were responsible for his deportation, so many years previously.

Jerzy pointed out that he himself had spent eighteen years in Siberian exile, but was married, with two sons and a daughter, also named Danuta. Over the ensuing couple of years, I have been in touch with this Danuta, initially via LinkedIn. Her father was trying to put together some information and photographs for me, although I can well understand that this process may have been emotional for him, perhaps too emotional, as writing this very personal account has been emotional for me. Overwhelmingly so at times. To this stress was added the horror of the Russian invasion. As I write this, I learn from his daughter that Jerzy has sadly died in Lviv. It must have seemed to him and his wife like a terrible history repeating itself at the hands of another psychotic dictator, just at the point where he might have anticipated a peaceful old age. My heart aches for him, his family and all those like him.

Another friend, writer and journalist Gerry Cassidy, wrote a story about my search for Danuta. This was published in Poland, resulting in more help from various sources. Most notably it put me in touch with Michał Zaleski, with his extensive and precise knowledge of Polish family history and resources. I was already in touch with Ewa Czerkawska, who has done so much to research the history of our family, and she has managed to ferret out more information than I would have believed possible.

Michał discovered that the original Danuta had, in fact, been Anna Danuta, named for her mother, which explained why searching for her online had been difficult. She was lucky to get a post war nursing scholarship to the US, one among twenty women chosen, with places so limited that only the most gifted got the opportunity. She had worked as a nurse throughout the war, so it's good to know that things started to go right for her. Now, her son Roman has sent me more information and a sheaf of photographs of the family. She returned to Poland in 1948, taking a job in a Warsaw hospital, marrying and moving to the Gdańsk area soon after. Her surviving son, Roman Kucharczyk, writes to me that his mother taught him to ski, to ice skate and to sledge. 'There were even sleigh rides,' he writes, and I realise with a little thrill of excitement that she must have learned all these things as a young woman in Dziedziłow, with my grandfather. She died, much too young, in 1960, when her sons, Roman and Witold, were only ten and eight years old.

I began this project by wanting to find out about my grand-father, Władysław Czerkawski. That line at the end of the film *Doctor Zhivago*, telling us that Lara is 'forgotten as a nameless number on a list which was later mislaid,' reminds me of Władysław and the conundrum of his life and character. Even now, I'm not at all sure that he truly loved any of the women in his life, but I find that line, and its echo in the film, profoundly moving. For so long after his death, and like so many others, he was a nameless number on a list that was later mislaid. When I was young, my father would speculate that he had 'been sent to Siberia' which was a catch-all for those many thousands of Poles, men, women and children, who had fallen foul of Stalin and who had been sent east, on cattle trucks or on foot, never to be seen or heard from again. Even when we were in contact with Łucja, she knew no more than we did, and nor did Wanda and Karol. From Russia, there had been a most profound silence. Then, when I did find out exactly what had become of him, and even where he was buried, it seemed essential that I know more about him than the bare facts of his birth and death, bringing him to life, as I so often bring charac-ters to life in my plays and novels. I had to tell his story, but in telling his story, I brought others to life as well.

My own father died in 1995, and my mother, truly lost without him, survived him by only three years. It was in the process of working on this book that I realised some-thing I wish I had been able to tell my father before he died. But I think he probably knew it as well as I do. There is a sense in which this whole book is a love story, or perhaps a series of them. If so, they are very grown-up love stories.

There is a man so much in love with his wife that he seeks to entice nightingales into the garden for her. A Polish girl absolutely determined to marry her Ukrainian lover. Wanda, falling in love and spending her whole life with the kind of artist of whom her father would have disapproved. My mother, meeting a foreigner, an 'alien', in a Leeds dance hall and falling head over heels in love with him. And there is my love for the grandfather I never knew, one of the last of the great Polish lancers. He was a warm, charming, but deeply flawed person who I now realise my father simply adored. It is there in every line he wrote about him, every tale he told me. More than that, the feeling was mutual. This has been one of the most difficult projects I have ever tackled, but in the end, it's simple. The true and abiding love of Władysław Czerkawski's life was his son Julian.

I wanted to see him come through our door, because the man my father described was somebody worth knowing. I had an English grandfather I knew and loved, but I also knew that there was another one, and I missed him. If he had ever walked through that door, I think he would have done what my father occasionally did, when he was feeling very Polish, and he knew the woman well enough: he would have kissed my hand, clicking his heels together in the accepted *szlachta* way and called me by the affection- ate diminutives of Katarzyna: Kasia, Katarzynka, Kasienka, Kasiunia. Eventually, I had to acknowledge that was never going to happen, so I have had to find other ways of getting to know him. Of 'acknowledging the dead'. In doing so, I have met and grown to love not just my grandfather, but a whole cast of characters who were once shadowy figures to me, inhabitants of a far country that once again is subject to terrible upheavals, not of its own making or desiring.

THE END

King Jan Sobieski
and Marysienka

To give the reader some idea of the old Polish commonwealth that seemed, to so many nineteenth- and twentieth-century Poles, like a lost 'Golden Age', it's interesting to take a brief look at King Jan Sobieski, his history and his world. You can judge for yourself, the nature of that lost world. Like most human enterprises, it was flawed, but fascinating.

According to legend, when the future King of Poland, Jan Sobieski, was born at Olesko in Eastern Poland, the infant was placed on top of a marble table, which promptly cracked in half. This seems to have been taken as a sign not of the general decrepitude of the castle, but that here was a child with an interesting future. Both were true. He would go on to lead the defence of Vienna against the Ottomans, and restore the Kingdom of Poland-Lithuania for what was destined to be its last great period of strength and influence, a period that as we have seen, would become a source of nostalgic longing for many of those who came after. The castle and its surrounding villages, predictably, continued to suffer the ravages of one battle after another, until the King, who was fond of the place, returned like Aragorn from the wars. His beloved wife seems to have been a prime mover in the castle's restoration, and together, the couple made good what had been destroyed. In the process, they amassed a fine collection of Polish artworks and artefacts of various kinds. As we shall see, this was by no means unusual at this time and in this place.

Sobieski was an intelligent, well educated, multilingual, ambitious and military-minded man who loved his wife even more than his country. To distraction, in fact. But then she too was intelligent, ambitious, beautiful and a Frenchwoman to boot. Since these qualities did not suit popular perceptions of the ideal woman, still less the ideal queen, i.e. an obedient and religious homemaker, she was not as popular with her subjects, nor with later commentators, as she so clearly was with her husband.

Marie Casimire Louise de La Grange d'Arquien was born in 1641, the daughter of an impoverished French nobleman, Henri de la Grange, and his wife Francoise. Poor Francoise bore Henri twelve children, one a year until her death in 1648, presumably of exhaustion. Only two daughters survived this marriage. Priapic Henri then married a widow named Charlotte, who gave birth to another six children, none of whom survived early childhood. Henri somewhat surprisingly – or perhaps not – became a Cardinal of the Roman Catholic Church from the age of 82, until his death in 1707 at the age of 94, outliving his daughter Marie by more than ten years.

Since the age of five, Marie Casimire had been living very comfortably indeed in the entourage of another French consort of not one but two Polish kings in succession: Louise-Marie Gonzaga, also of Nevers, later Queen Louise-Marie of Poland, where she was known as Ludovika Maria. The Queen first brought Marie Casimire to Poland when she was five years old, but then sent the child back to France to finish her education, and again welcomed her to Poland circa 1652 or 53 when, according to the aristocratic customs of the time, she would have been of marriageable age.

The two women seem to have been as close as mother and daughter, which is hardly surprising, given their long association. In fact given their mutual origins in Nevers, I found myself indulging in a little wild speculation about the relationship, only to discover that there were plenty of rumours about Marie Casimire's origins at the time. The fact is that an engaging and bright child, who grew to womanhood at the court, would have been treated very much as a foster daughter, especially since Louise Marie's own two children did not survive infancy, a daughter dying aged one in 1651 and a son at only a few months old, early in 1652. The coincidence of Marie Casimire's return to Poland around the same time may have had a lot to do with a grieving Louise Marie desiring the comfort and companionship of a girl who she looked on as a daughter. On the other hand, Henri's eighteen children (pretty much one a year, with a year off for mourning) might indicate a man of healthy, not to say promiscuous appetites.

Earlier in her life, and in spite of her physical comforts, Queen Louise-Marie had had an unhappy time as a pawn in various fraught political machinations, all of them unsurprisingly involving struggles for power between unscrupulous men. She and her protegee were intelligent, interested in politics, and they had plans. Neither of them received a good press from the men surrounding them, a denigration which continues to this day, in a truly dreadful

Wikipedia entry which describes Marie Casimire as a 'hard, arrogant, self centred woman'. During her lifetime, she was often compared unfavourably with the saintly and highly educated Queen Christina of Sweden, although even she was accused of driving the country towards bankruptcy with her extravagance. As ever, intelligent women who refuse to be kind and fit into the moulds prescribed for them find themselves slated by those men who come after. Clever, forthright Marie Casimire was never going to fit in with the Polish ideal of the obedient housewife presiding over the domestic and religious sphere of her limited life.

In 1658, at the age of seventeen, Marie Casimire was married, perhaps at the instigation of the Queen, to a wealthy nobleman, called Jan Zamoyski. Jan already had a reputation as a libertine. The Queen herself knew all about the unhappy consequences of pressure exerted on a woman to marry the right, powerful man. It doesn't seem to have prevented her from trying to exert the same pressure on her beloved Marie Casimire, although Zamoyski, a reasonably young man from a powerful family, would have been seen as the perfect marriage candidate for the Queen's favourite, albeit not from a Polish point of view. Zamoyski was the principal heir of Zamość, a wealthy renaissance town founded in the previous century by his grandfather, also Jan Zamoyski. This is a distinguished family which shares the Jelita coat of arms with my own, although we never shared their wealth. Marie bore her husband four children in quick succession, none of whom survived infancy.

Much of the information of this time and place, this milieu, involves an interweaving of plotting and angling for power. Nothing changes. If the Queen was playing politics by encouraging the alliance of her protégée with the powerful Zamoyski family, Marie Casimire didn't seem to mind too much. Not at this stage, anyway, although the honeymoon period – if it could ever be called that – didn't last very long. Zamoyski's portrait, which may not do him justice, depicts a haughty and plumply self-conscious soldier, who looks older than his years, since he was thirty when the couple married and not yet forty when he died, unexpectedly by some accounts, and with no surviving legitimate children. There would be dark hints of foul play, but we should remind ourselves again that, as an intelligent and forthright Frenchwoman, Marie was far from popular, especially with those whose ambitions clashed with her own. Much like our tabloid press, there would have been plenty of influential people who would have been only too happy to brief against her, to spread lies and rumours. In her various portraits she manages to be both buxom and elfish at the same time, with a cloud of gorgeous dark hair, sensuous lips, and a knowing stare. In short, she's astoundingly pretty. Zamoyski must have thought himself very lucky in his choice of bride.

As was the custom, Marie had left the court after her marriage. Her husband was reluctant to bring her back to Warsaw, even when he himself was there, but she was hungry for information from that city. She was also, of course, a regular correspondent of the Queen. And the Queen was hungry for the kind of useful gossip that she could not easily get from those closest to her, without arousing suspicions of her motives. Women must find other ways. In this case, those ways involved a third party known to both women: Jan Sobieski.

When he and Marie first met, Sobieski was a couple of years younger than Zamoyski, an unmarried, swashbuckling captain of the Royal Standard Bearers. Marie had probably been aware of him since she was a child. There are romantic tales of their love at first sight, but these are probably exaggerated, and there is little sign of it in their earlier correspondence, when she was a married woman, living very discontentedly elsewhere and pressuring him for information. His later portraits show him, like Zamoyski, running to fat somewhat, but you can see that he must have been a handsome not to say dashing man when younger. There's one striking picture of him with dark hair, a fine dark moustache, and big dark eyes, that gives you some idea of how attractive he would have seemed to a clever young woman, used to the mental swordplay of court life, bored by domesticity, bored by her surroundings and without even the distraction of surviving children.

Their initial correspondence seems to have involved a combination of Marie's genuine desire to know what was going on at court, coupled with her growing status as middlewoman on behalf of her other correspondent: Louise-Marie. It's clear that the Queen wanted to be kept abreast of military and political developments as much as Marie did herself and what better way to avert suspicion than to forward Sobieski's information via Marie Casimire in Zamość, under cover of a string of friendly letters between the Queen and her protegee? All this was clearly a secretive, not to say dangerous, business and Marie often cautions circumspection in her correspondence, while Sobieski finds writing so many incautious letters to a powerful man's restless wife a fraught undertaking, and not at all one that he is sure is wise. This hesitancy infuriates his fiery correspondent who, of course, has the backing of the queen.

What is Sobieski to do?

'You are a foolish man if you take it for granted that your correspondent will trouble herself to write to you, while you spend your time only on pleasure,' Marie Casimire tells him, furiously, with a certain amount of jealousy at his 'pleasure' too, one can't help noticing. She is beginning to feel proprietorial about him. She instructs him to send such letters as are to be forwarded to the queen sealed with red wax. He must use different coloured waxes for other letters, so that she will know which is which. Both know that any letters addressed directly to the queen by Sobieski might be stolen or otherwise tampered with. Other factions at court would suspect him (rightly) of spying. But, given the lowly status of women, few would suspect a correspondence between Queen Louise-Marie and her young lady-in-waiting of being anything but domestic. Female fripperies. What they made of an ongoing correspondence between libertine Zamoyski's young wife and a handsome soldier is anybody's guess, but it was either dismissed as a mere flirtation between the standard bearer and the beautiful Zamoyska, or condemned as somehow 'typical' of a Frenchwoman. All the same, Marie sends Sobieski parcels of the required wax, which suggests a woman who likes to be in control. She also tells him to burn her letters after reading them. Little of her side of the correspondence from this time survives, so he probably did as he was told.

Predictably, perhaps, the correspondence soon turned from one of purely business-like relaying of information, to familiarity, friendship, and a growing affection. The pair facilitated the necessary secrecy by inventing code names for the various protagonists, as well as for each other. For a while they seem to have indulged in a form of epistolatory courtly love, coupled with a rather acid commentary on the court and their respective families. Marie never abandoned her own political machinations and ambitions. The necessary pseudonyms were not kind, even when referring to Marie's husband (they called him, variously, Fool, Horse and Mackerel) and his sister, who is sometimes referred to as Double Bass or Baking Tin. Intriguingly, there is a surviving and rather grand baking tin at Wilanow in Warsaw, all curves and gleaming copper. Other courtiers were Crocodile, Slipper, Sponge and Apple, fascinating identities to which we seem to have no key.

It's soon clear that Marie loves Sobieski more than she loves her husband, to the extent that in 1661, they make secret promises of love and fidelity in the Carmelite Church in Warsaw, a proceeding which is reported matter-of-factly, but seems extraordinary even from a twenty-first-century perspective: a couple, one of whom is married, promising fidelity with the blessing of the church. It's worth noting that the queen herself had a long association with the Carmelites, having promised her firstborn daughter, Maria Anna, to them. There's a disturbing portrait in existence of the tiny toddler in a Carmelite habit, but the child escaped this dubious fate by dying suddenly at thirteen months. Perhaps the queen facilitated the secret vows. Perhaps she was captivated by the romance, by an intrigue that still enthrals the contemporary reader.

Marie, meanwhile, was lending Jan Sobieski copies of French pastoral romances from her husband's library. Sobieski was enchanted by these tales of 'shepherd romance' in which the lovers would not just converse, whenever they could, but would explore intimately but restrainedly, the very nature of their love, by means of a regular and elegant correspondence. The shepherdess was supposed to remain aloof, while the shepherd was imbued with a restrained passion for the beloved, a passion which was sublimated in letters. This was an appealing game for a while, but not, perhaps, one that could be prolonged indefinitely. Thereafter, the couple seem to have corresponded under sentimental pseudonyms. One is irresistibly reminded of the way in which more than a hundred years later, Scottish poet Robert Burns and pretty (but also unhappily married) Nancy McLehose would indulge in a passionate and totally unrealistic correspondence as Clarinda and Sylvander, fondly indulging in rural fantasies of the shepherd and shepherdess – a far cry from the realities of farming life. In fact one of the names Sobieski chose was indeed Sylvander. Unlike Burns and his Clarinda, however, whose fantasy was interrupted by the all too real birth of another set of twins to the poet's lawful wife, Jan and Marie chose to convert fantasy into reality.

Occasionally, Marie escaped from Zamość to see her parents in France, perhaps to relieve the pressure of what had turned out to be an unhappy marriage, complicated by an increasing passion for the much more charming Sobieski. In April 1662, Marie headed for Paris, taking with her quantities of gold, silver, jewellery and Zamoyski's servants. To be fair, her husband seemed to be having a high old time in Warsaw. Marie bought herself a very fancy bed, so that she could indulge in the aristocratic fashion of receiving people while lying thereon, looking interestingly sickly and frail, no matter how strong she might be in reality. This was perhaps a bridge, or a bed, too far for the forthright Sobieski, who seemed to have more conventional ideas of the uses of beds, albeit not just for sleeping.

When Zamoyski died in 1665, Marie and Jan married with somewhat indecent haste, in the middle of that same year, without respecting the conventional year of mourning for a widow. This was almost certainly because of pressure on Jan to marry elsewhere, a pressure which he was determined to resist. By now, he was certain who he wanted in his bed and in his life, and he was not to be diverted. In 1667, some time after the wedding and after the devastating death of her friend and mentor, Queen Louise-Marie, a pregnant Marie departed for France again, for the sake of her health, and the couple's first child, Jakub, was born very respectably towards the end of 1667. The following year, Louise-Marie's heartbroken husband, Jan Casimir, abdicated and also moved to France.

It seems as though Marie would have liked for herself and Sobieski to settle down in France too, but it was not to be and, nothing if not a realist, she knew it. Sobieski was growing ever more popular in Poland, both for his military accomplishments and his love for his native land. He was an attractive and capable character, and it must have become clear to Marie that a return to France was not on the agenda. In 1669, Michał Wiśniowiecki, Jan Zamoyski's nephew, was elected King, but Marie was not a supporter. When he died from severe food poisoning in 1673, she celebrated the subsequent election of her husband, Jan Sobieski III, as monarch and judged it to be her personal success as much as his. There were again rumours that the food poisoning had been actual poisoned food, but in the absence of proof, the simplest explanation is probably the correct one.

It seems to have been a love match and one that lasted.

Marie, known by the diminutive of her name Marysienka, not always used affectionately outside her marriage, gets a bad press as a 'meddlesome wife'. When Jan was elected King of Poland in 1674, we are told that his wife made herself unpopular, largely it seems because of her support for an alliance between Poland and France. As a Frenchwoman by birth, her loyalties must have been divided. France was still, in some sense, home.

Sobieski's most famous victory was his defeat of the invading Ottoman Army at the gates of Vienna, in 1683, in which the Polish-Lithuanian Commonwealth had lent its considerable military strength to the Hapsburgs in defence of that city. Poles were celebrated cavalrymen and at least some of their fearsome reputation rested on the extraordinary Winged Hussars, with their terrifying eagle feather armour. Jointly commanding German and Polish troops, Sobieski defeated a well equipped Turkish army. Less widely appreciated, however, is the undoubted admiration that already existed between the Polish cavalry and their Ottoman foes, or at least an admiration for their weaponry, their trappings and their costumes. Sobieski had brought military fashion to the court, and that military fashion was Turkish, both in dress and weaponry, which was deemed to be superior, largely because it was. This was so much the case that the Poles and the Ottomans were similarly attired, and at the Battle of Vienna, the Poles were instructed to wear distinctive cockades to distinguish them from the enemy. The Ottoman army was splendidly accoutred, and the booty that fell into Sobieski's hands, from the battle of Vienna alone, was spectacular. '*Fort jolies et fort riches*' he described these things in the inevitable letter to his wife, remarking that he hadn't yet had time to look through everything. I expect Marie Casimire was not averse to sifting through the loot with her beloved husband.

In the 1970s, I visited my cousin Teresa Kossak and her partner Andrzej Lipka, in their tiny Warsaw apartment, and listened to Andrzej describing his passionate (and wholly infectious) attachment to the Ottoman inspired weaponry and other items that had been appropriated by the Poles throughout the seventeenth century, and then used as models for their own weaponry. I was very young, and don't think I quite understood just how extraordinary this was, at the time. It just struck me that he was describing a deep appreciation of something that may have been long past, and mostly long lost, but was as immediate to him as it would have been to Sobieski and his knights. He found these things utterly beautiful, and could explain why, in such thrilling and knowledgeable terms, that you understood at once how fine they were.

The Poles may have fought the Ottomans, but they just loved their enemies' possessions, to the extent that they adopted their weaponry, their style of dress, their passion for ornament and luxury, coupled with an intense appreciation of Islamic arts and crafts that was not at all understood in the rest of Western Europe. I suppose now it would be condemned as cultural appropriation, and there certainly was a fair amount of appropriation involved. Not for them the destructive tendencies of later armies. Human beings were still fair game, of course, but works of art were not to be trifled with. And certainly not to be destroyed if they could be seized.

This enthusiasm for Ottoman acquisitions was fulfilled in peacetime through trade and in time of war through less benign means. Flemish tapestries were replaced by wonderful Islamic hangings, finely ornamented weapons were collected and given pride of place on the walls of old Polish manor houses. The *szlachta* adopted the Ottoman style, as surely as an attractive fashion will spread among young people today. The traditional 'Sarmatian' costume was seen as patriotically Polish, with its long skirted coat, trousers tucked into leather boots, and beautifully embroidered Turkish fabric belts, known as *kontusz* sashes, i.e. 'robe sashes'. The prized sashes were decorated with rich embroidery and gold thread, and were essentially a fashion statement, their possession an indicator of wealth. After the Battle of Chocim, Sobieski acquired, among the spoils of war, a silk embroidery studded with two thousand emeralds and rubies, which he loved so much that he used it as a ceremonial horse cloth during his coronation. We may think, from a twenty-first-century perspective, that using jewelled embroideries as horse cloths denotes a certain lack of respect, but remember that Poles were a people for whom horsemanship was little short of a religion, a passion for horses that had hardly abated even in the twentieth century, when my father was born. Later, Sobieski presented it to the Grand Duke of Tuscany, who described it as a 'thing of barbaric magnificence'. As a textile collector myself, albeit in a small way, I find my mouth watering at such a thing of beauty. Most Polish aristocrats of that age simply saw the magnificence and cared not a jot about the barbarism.

Conspicuous consumption seems to have been the order of the day for those who could afford it. But this seldom involved acquiring and hoarding coin. Instead, wealth involved jewelled items, art, finely crafted weapons of all kinds, furs, horsecloths, decorated saddlery, even lengths of gold and silver embroidered cloth. Among the *szlachta*, a coat might be heavily embroidered with gold or silver thread and fastened with jewelled buttons. On a normal day, Sobieski might wear a considerable quantity of precious jewels about his person, while on truly ceremonial occasions, his sumptuous dress would involve riches beyond the dreams of avarice. He was a large man, which was just as well, since his costumes must have weighed him and his poor horse down.

'The Sarmatian lifestyle was a unique growth produced by a cross-pollination between Catholic high Baroque and

Ottoman Culture' writes MSW in an enlightening and incisive article on the 'History, Poland' website. It certainly bore little resemblance to the ethic of puritanism, discipline and self improvement that was growing across Western Europe at this time. Polish culture was dramatic, ostentatious, flamboyant in the extreme. It may have seemed utterly outrageous from the outside, looking in: a theatrical performance. But it was also unusually tolerant too, involving as it did, an amalgam of two or more essentially warring cultures that spawned a certain amount of respect between individuals who should have been sworn enemies. Jan Sobieski's English physician wrote 'It is certain had we in England but the third part of their liberty, we could not live together without cutting one another's throats.' The liberty may have been more performative than actual, and the poor would have been too busy surviving to participate, but for a time at least, it worked.

Throughout their marriage, Jan Sobieski and Marie Casimire had thirteen children of whom nine were either stillborn, or died in infancy or very soon after. The fact that we know that at least two of the girls who didn't survive were given loving pet names, Barbelune, who died aged four, and La Mannone, who was only two when she died, suggests that infant mortality would have been as devastating then as now, albeit far more commonplace for kings and commoners alike. We also know that Marie and her second husband continued to write love letters to each other, and that the King often consulted his wife about decisions, both domestic and political. Alongside those concerning politics and preferment, one of her many projects involved the restoration of the castle at Olesko where Jan had been born, for which he retained great affection and which became a holiday bolt hole for the couple, albeit a luxurious one. At least some of the artefacts that made it so comfortable must have come from those 'very pretty, very rich' things harvested from the defeated Turks. Sobieski though, continued to see his wife as the prettiest of all.

'To the only delight of my heart and soul, the most beautiful and dearest Marysienka, I embrace you, the most beautiful woman in the world, and kiss you a million times!' he wrote to her when they were apart. There's a strong streak of romance in many Poles that often comes as a surprise to anyone not familiar with the nation. Even in smoky down-to-earth 1940s Leeds, when my refugee father was courting my Leeds Irish mother, he inscribed 'to Kathleen, from ever loving Julian' to her, on a little wooden musical box. I have it still, the writing faded but characteristic of the man and his family.

Acknowledgements

It is no exaggeration to say that without the help of a great number of people and organisations who were beyond generous with their time and expertise, over a number of years, I doubt if I could have finished this book. They have given me invaluable assistance in finding out much more about my family than I would have thought possible. I can never thank them enough for their generosity and understanding. Among them, I must name Ewa Czerkawska, Michał Zaleski, Iwona Piasecka, her son Tom Piasecki and Gerry Cassidy for their indefatigable assistance. Their contribution is beyond price. Profound thanks also to Jerzy Hanakowski and his daughter Dana, Roman Kucharczyk, Ewa Cherner, Neal Ascherson, Valery Podolynyy, Nadija Maciuk, Michał Zawisza and my friend and fellow writer Olga Wojtas for reassurance and editorial assistance. Thanks too to my friend Dr Alison Bell, for advice and support.

Helpful organisations include the Austrian State Archive, the Austrian Parliamentary Library, the Library of the Jagiellonian University in Kraków, the helpful staff of the Bergen Belsen Museum, the equally helpful staff at the APC Polish Enquiries office of the MOD and perhaps most of all the brilliantly informative and supportive Kresy Siberia Facebook Group and its related sites.

No longer with us, but contributors in all kinds of ways to this long project, I bless and acknowledge the two brave

Tadeusz Czerkawskis and their respective families, my much loved Aunt Wanda, Uncle Karol and Cousin Teresa Kossak and above all, my dear father, Julian Władysław Czerkawski, who wrote so much down for me at a time when he was far from well.

Finally, many thanks as ever to my husband Alan Lees, to our son Charles, and to all at Saraband, especially Yennah Smart, for perceptive and helpful editing, to Ellie Croston and most of all to Sara Hunt for patiently bearing with me through what has been a long and difficult project.

Select Reading List

Neal Ascherson, *The Death of the Fronsac*, Head of Zeus, 2018

Zosia Biegus, *Polish Resettlement Camps in England and Wales*, P B Software, 2013

The Black Book of Poland, The Polish Ministry of Information, G P Putnam's Sons, New York, 1942

Cygan and Skalski, *Poland, in Defence of Freedom 1939-1945*, Warsaw 2005

Norman Davies, *Rising '44*, Macmillan 2003

Julie Hrykiel, *Konrad's War and Peace*, Friends of Poland, 1994

Teresa Kossak, *Kossak Nieznany*, Panstwowy Instytut Wydawniczy 2013

Evan McGilvray, *Anders' Army: General Władysław Anders and the Polish Second Corps 1941-46*, Pen and Sword Military, 2018

Stefan Mekarski, *Lwów, A Page of Polish History*, Kolo Lwówian, London 1991

Adam Mickiewicz, *Pan Tadeusz* (English verse translated by Kenneth R Mackenzie) Polish Cultural Foundation 1986

Kazimierz Olszański, *Wojciech Kossak*, Warsaw 1976

Mary Pińinska, *The Polish Kitchen*, Macmillan 1990

Timothy Snyder, *Bloodlands*, Vintage 2010

Zbigniew Wawer, *From Buzuluk to Monte Cassino*, Warsaw 2009

Stanislaw Wyspiański, *Acropolis, the Wawel Plays*, Glagoslav Publications B.V

Adam Zamoyski, *The Polish Way*, John Murray 1987

Adam Zamoyski, *Poland: A History, Harper Press*, 2009

WEBSITES

https://culture.pl/en/article/polish-tangos-the-unique-inter-war-soundtrack-to-polands-independence

https://polishhistory.pl/john-iii-sobieski-and-marysienka/

https://culture.pl/en/artist/stanislaw-wyspianski

https://www.1944.pl/en/article/the-warsaw-rising-mu-seum,4516.html

https://www.wilanow-palac.pl/jan_sobieski_s_military_and_political_career.html

https://en.wikipedia.org/wiki/Battle_of_Lemberg_(1918)

https://bergen-belsen.stiftung-ng.de/

https://discover-ukraine.info/places/western-ukraine/lviv/83

https://www.familysearch.org/en/wiki/Poland_Websites

https://kresy-siberia.org/

https://www.facebook.com/historicalcolors

https://www.facebook.com/groups/3625556537551157   (Polish Heritage)

https://pl.wikipedia.org/wiki/Feliks_Zbigniew_Machnowski

https://swoopingeagle.com/home/research/how-to-get-polish-military-records-from-the-uk-mod/

The Czerkawski siblings at Meryszczow, 1926.

THE AUTHOR

Catherine Czerkawska is a critically acclaimed writer of long and short fiction, non-fiction and plays. Her novels include *The Curiosity Cabinet, The Physic Garden, Bird of Passage* and *The Jewel*, about the life of Robert Burns's wife, Jean Armour.

In 2019 Contraband published *A Proper Person to be Detained*, an intriguing exploration of family history that takes us from nineteenth-century Ireland to the industrial heartlands of England and Scotland. *The Last Lancer* follows this personal account with an exploration of Catherine's family history on the 'other side of the tree'.

Catherine's stage plays include *Wormwood*, about the Chernobyl disaster, and *Quartz*, both commissioned by Edinburgh's Traverse Theatre. She has also written more than 100 hours of drama for BBC Radio 4.

Catherine spent four years as Royal Literary Fund Writing Fellow at the University of the West of Scotland, and when not writing, she collects and deals in the antique textiles that occasionally find their way into her fiction.